# Corporate America:
# Surviving Your Journey Towards Success

# Corporate America:
# Surviving Your Journey Towards Success

### Nichel Anderson

Writer's Showcase
New York  Lincoln  Shanghai

Corporate America: Surviving Your Journey Towards Success

Writer's Showcase
an imprint of iUniverse, Inc.

For information address:
iUniverse
2021 Pine Lake Road, Suite 100
Lincoln, NE 68512
www.iuniverse.com

ISBN: 0-595-26818-8

Printed in the United States of America

# DEDICATION

*I dedicate the purpose and the mission*
*of this book to my beloved angel: my son Malachi*

# CONTENTS

# FOREWORD

Stressed out again? Caught in a catch 20 by 20 corporate situation? Thinking about quitting and going to another company in search of greener pastures? Bills are due and a call is coming in for you to accept that car loan? Your boss is at your desk because he/she doesn't understand the contents of Mr. Williams' file due to a co-worker blaming you for the messed up file. Well, I have been in these familiar situations due to the twelve years I have been in Corporate America, in which, has provided me with the experience of gaining exceptional interpersonal skills, effective verbal and written communication leading to successful situations.

I decided to write about the ups and downs of Corporate America because of my own challenges with co-workers and upper management struggle to survive the ride of the big bull of big business. I began to master over time the effective way in getting results with upper management and your immediate team members. In turn, I became an effective corporate team player. I have outlined the many lessons here in a context that is presented in order for your journey through Corporate America to be a successful one. Even if you choose not to excel to management level this collaboration of pertinent strategies will make your journey through Corporate America a rewarding one, for the new breed just starting out—to the veterans of managing office politics.

Life is a journey and Corporate America challenges you, teach you, and even if allowed it could at times crush you. However, my initiative is to show you how to effectively maneuver the often-tidal waves of Corporate America…leading you to success.

And so it is.

Nichel Anderson

# ACKNOWLEDGMENTS

I would like to thank all of the encouraging moments I had with the many co-workers and managers; I had encountered working for in Corporate America. I would like to say a special thank you to my older sister, Bridgett Anderson, for listening to my many stressful conflicts at work and being so supportive. You are my very best friend. I would like to say thank you to my older brother, Rahseem Xamir, for hugging me with supporting words when I wanted to quit so many times—and thank you so much for making me laugh by calling me often at my jobs to see how I was doing (really to see if I'm still there). A thank you to my Dad, for making me smile often when you shared your jokes with Rasheem on my ability to stand up to adversity and dilemmas in Corporate America. Also, a needed thank you to Michele Hriciso for emailing me back and forth with encouragement during my many difficult situations. A special thank you to Mr. Larry T. Richardson for giving me a positive and a higher understanding on the corporate existence, I really appreciated your advice.

*All the best,*

Nichel Anderson

**Photo credits on book cover:** (From left to right) IvaneHope Oliependio, Richard Bryant, Nichel Anderson, Andrea Means, and Stephanie Cooks

**Photographer:** Gennice Hamilton

**The important components of a company that has and sustains a successful relationship with their customers and employees are:**

*Communication*: The ability to express oneself effectively to others that will enlighten, explain, and compliment the foresaid initiative for the department. Effective communication is both verbally and written where no misinterpretation is present only a solid and firm foundation of the cause for the initiative and effect leading to detail ways the initiative will be implemented.

*Conflict:* Talking with the other party in a calm non-hostile environment i.e. conference room, to reach a suitable resolution for both parties. And not being afraid to apologize if the error in judgment or action was on your part, instead, the individual will move forward towards a resolution and sustain strong interpersonal skills.

*Culture:* Understanding and honoring people with diversity will lead to strong interpersonal skills because we will watch what we say or do to others different than ourselves.

*Technology:* Having continued training seminars and classes for increase learning from software and systems will allow employees becoming an effective player, and employees and employers will gain great advancement in their career fields as well as accomplishing the initiatives of the company.

PART ONE

# DEFINING YOUR MESSAGE

# CHAPTER 1

# Your Attitude

Nichel Anderson:

*"I wanted my ideas and opinions to be heard. After my firm statement to the group, the project leader still refused to see my proposed resolution. My manager instead continued to talk, absently refusing to hear the growing concerns of what a mess our future daily job tasks will be if this initiative goes through. I wanted to scream."*

Many times we have been in this position in corporate life; I have counted the times where I thought I could have handled this situation differently to reach my objective. Oftentimes, I chose to ride against the tidal wave of corporate politics with no respect to its unique identity.

Corporate America is an entity with its own boundaries of influential power. Corporate America is a living and breathing group of big players producing big business that dramatically affects the economy of the United States. From the large conglomerate to the mom-and-pop businesses, the inner politics of Corporate America must be understood and respected in order to be an effective player in this journey.

This respect is an *understanding* that being an effective player is crucial because it provides for your very livelihood; mastering the makeup of Corporate America will enlighten you and lead you to achieving success. The function of the corporate structure will be better understood once you learn to respect it as the powerhouse that controls all measures of that business as well as the components making up that business.

Adapting an exterior of approachability and having a good attitude will enable those around you to lead you further in your career. In my previous example, I felt I was given no respect. I even at times had a fierce facial expression; as a determined player I was ready to push my ideas in order to be heard.

Our attitudes are the foundation of success in Corporate America because it allows the opportunity to reach the company foresaid goals. It is your business card, an opportunity to navigate successfully through your challenging journey. Why is your attitude so important? Do you really need to master your emotional balance and maintain a calm exterior? What are the effects of having a good attitude or a bad one?

Let's begin to uncover the integral parts of gaining what we need for the journey:

## Why Is Your Attitude So Important?

A good attitude can guarantee an individual to go far in Corporate America. You are an individual with ideas, likes and dislikes, but you are working within a team in a business. Your attitude is crucial to helping the team reach its objectives.

In order to obtain a good attitude and keep your energy in balance, you have to do some personal evaluation. It is hard because most of us would rather lay out our demands and be heard by those that have the power to set our plans in motion. We miss the lesson that yelling doesn't get you anywhere but out the door. We listen to our own needs and are bewildered that no one else gets it.

When we are labeled, we are even angrier. Sometimes we become vengeful and vindictive when we leave the company, naming all the dirty deeds you witnessed and gossiping to leave behind viruses that infect the corporate morale.

To keep from engaging in this harmful behavior, we must master the technique of being centered. We must come to terms with what is really bothering us. Probably 9 times out of 10 it is our personal lives that are in turmoil, and we bring it to the workplace. Corporate America has no mammas or daddies to help us get over our years of wounds; it is an entity whose primary objective is to generate a profit and stay on top of its chosen field.

Accepting the core concept of cooperation can help you to be a more effective player and become successful within the corporate framework. You just have to decide to work on the issues that are preventing you from seeing the big picture. You have to begin right now to adjust your personality and heal those wounds in order to focus completely and contribute honestly to the job at hand. It won't be easy because most of us are comfortable; it is easier to leave wounds be. But if we allow the wounds not to heal, we open ourselves up to explosive confrontations with the very people we need to succeed with at work.

Be honest. Be sincere on your quest, and you shall be successful in your journey.

## HOW TO BEGIN YOUR SELF-ANALYSIS

* Have a mentor or someone that you can trust to help you evaluate your strengths and weaknesses. Ask them to provide an up-front analysis of your attitude.

* You will need to get a journal. Use this journal to write down your daily experiences at work; underneath your recollections write down what you would have done differently. You will be using your journal to record the patterns of interaction with your co-workers, team members and upper management. At the end of day, preferably, or at the end of the week go back and reflect on these experiences. Keep in mind several questions as you read these passages:

   1. Did I represent the best attitude while discussing the agenda with this person?
   2. Was I really listening to what was being said before I jumped in?
   3. Were my eyes alert during the discussion and not arched in contempt?
   4. Was my attitude, prior to the incident, due to an argument with my spouse, boyfriend, etc.?
   5. Am I already angry before talking to this person?
   6. Did the discussion end in a good note?
   7. What can I do better next time?

* Learn to be honest about what *you* contribute to the situation in your work environment. Stop blaming others; make sure your approach to others is free of anger, resentments, jealousy and other past occurrences still plaguing your mind, heart and soul.

\* Be aware of what sets you off and use your journal tracking to help you monitor your progress. If a pattern persists where most of the outbursts are rooted in personal issues and not business related incidents, you will definitely need to consult a counselor to help you get your personal life back on track. The counselor will be able to assist you healing those deep wounds that lead you to be angry making you unapproachable.

## Do You Really Need To Master Your Emotional Balance Towards Calmness?

Absolutely. This is the true test of our successfulness in the journey through corporate life. Years ago, I sabotaged myself by not taking the necessary steps to calm down. I chose to react hastily rather than to respond with calmness. It takes time to master this calm exterior but the pay off will be well worth it.

Allowing balance in our lives at work provides us with the ability to focus on the task at hand. There are always projects, assignments, and pending phone calls stacking up that we must get done. When duties pile up and we feel overwhelmed, we carry more stress on our backs. When we get into a heated situation, our blood pressure rises, our eyes dilate in contempt, and we start slamming things on our desks. And then it seems like the unfinished duties are staring at you: not caring that you are upset.

## TAKING STEPS TO REACH CALMNESS

a. Breathe. It is very important because breathing calms your heart and mind—the vital parts of your well being to regroup and not surrender to negative energy.

b. Take in deep breaths and then exhale. Pay attention to the rhythm of your breathing. Make sure it is soothing and not rushed.

c. Repeat these breathing exercises as you count to ten.

d. Leave the building to stand outside to regroup.

e. Talk to someone you trust who will listen and not neglect your confidence.

f. Try to concentrate or start working on another task to move forward.

g. Write down your thoughts. Don't worry about the spelling or grammar; the key is to get your emotions out of your heart and onto paper, and to become calmer while doing it.

h. Read a spiritual scripture or a favorite quote to get you centered and focused. You might even say a prayer; in this stage of the game, spiritual grounding can only help guide you through the wilderness of Corporate America.

These steps are geared toward effectively managing your emotions in order for you to steer clear of negative energy. This is crucial on your quest in surviving your journey to success. In addition, these techniques will help provide you to define your true desire—to be a vital member of the team and the company.

## What Are The Effects Of Your Attitude?

With a good attitude, you are guaranteed a wonderful day at work, even if the other party is the aggressor. Your co-workers, managers, and customers will be drawn to you. More opportunities to prosper professionally will be at your feet and you will feel empowered in allowing yourself to dictate your happiness. Individuals will listen to your every word and encourage others to do so as well because your presentation of a good attitude transcends negative perceptions.

If you have a bad attitude, you are guaranteed to be labeled, not chosen for that big project and approached differently. When we place ourselves in the mode of anger, jealousy and frustration, we allow ourselves to be labeled. In Corporate America that is at the top of the list of not being a team player. You will be unable to get that position you so desired, work with that particular colleague who could lead your career to a higher level, etc. When you are labeled with having a bad attitude, it can also lead you to losing your job. No one that is success driven adds fuel to the fire of an incident.

All managers and senior managers would agree that having a great attitude is essential to success. Upper management will listen and you will be *heard*; your smile and choice of words will present the best constructive criticism concerning the project, and in turn your choices will be implemented. *Always remember to choose wisely.*

I have posed some pertinent questions to some colleagues as well as employees from different levels of large corporations, small businesses and online companies. I wanted to assess the effects of having a good attitude and having a bad attitude.

### 5 Questions posed to different team players in Corporate America:

A) First recall an experience of having a bad attitude and the *results* of your actions.

*Jason Pamer, Editorial Director of Suite101.com:*

"When the company I currently work for, Suite101.com, was first starting out, I sometimes became frustrated with the lack of security that a start-up company offers. During periods of difficulty I found myself focusing too much on the potential pitfalls of working for a start-up rather than embracing the opportunities that it offered. When times were good, I thrived on the higher risk-reward atmosphere. When capital funding and other issues looked bleak, it was hard not to focus on the negatives.

The result of my seesaw attitude was that the valuable experience and knowledge I was gaining was at times lost on me. It made the downswings in Suite101.com's fortunes more stressful and worrisome than necessary. Instead of being completely focused on helping the company overcome these obstacles, I found myself distracted by the misconceived notion that working for a secure, established company would save me from these ups and downs."

**\*\*\*\*\*\*\*\*\*\***

### Nathaniel Alexander, Fuel System Technician Key, Northrop Grumman Inc.

*"While working in Corporate America, I ran across many different attitudes. Those attitudes often affected mine. Not only the attitude but also the differences of how one sees you; that may be different than what one would expect. When you carry yourself in a way that demands respect, people are often intimidated by your positive attractiveness. While working, a conflict occurred between a lead worker and me. I was talking to a coworker when my lead approached me and said he was tired of seeing me talk to coworkers when I should be working. I replied, if smokers can take ten to fifteen minutes per hour smoke breaks, I could talk to someone if I want to. He later came back and said I need to do what I'm told and gets to work, in a very loud tone.*

*Our supervisor wanted to know what was going on, so he asked the lead to explain. He later asked me to explain my side. Our supervisor came to the conclusion that there was nothing wrong with me talking to co-workers as long as it didn't interfere with my work schedule or someone else's schedule. It was also said that smokers were taking breaks that were unauthorized and it was happening much too often, and they weren't meeting the work schedule. I determined that I really needed to leave because it was only the blacks that the attention was on for talking and we were the ones producing most of the work.*

*Resentment was also part of my problem because I spoke out about some of the problems. I made it known that if the problems don't go away neither will I. Later I was transferred to another site close to home, so it worked out in a way but things were left unfinished. I'm now at a new site and we try to address situations head on. Problems will always exist, but it's how those situations are handled that makes it worthwhile."*

\*\*\*\*\*\*\*\*\*

*- Angela Stephens, Quality Analyst at Aetna US Healthcare*

"I was leaving for the day and still had quite a bit of work on my desk, so I told my co-workers to take from the top of the stack if they run out work. However, when I returned back the next day, most of my work was gone, and all I was left with was hard cases. It was so obvious that someone picked through my work and took out all the easy cases. I was furious because this person didn't care about the others not meeting their production. So, I went around and asked each of my team members who took work from my desk. It turned out to be a particular team member who had came from a different area, with an already name of a troublemaker for herself. I approached her, and we got in a confrontational incident. Our team leader was informed of the argument and matter, and the manager stated that she would handle it appropriately.

The details of how it was handled are vague, but what I do recall is the lesson I learned now, as I am older, in Corporate America. And that is that I have chosen my battles and that using my anger to handle matters is not the answer. I look back at that incident and see where I went wrong, I should not have chosen to get so upset to cause a scene that could have gotten me fired. And that would have been really sad since I tried for months to get into this major company in our town and to lose my job and opportunities because of my anger—even if the co-worker was at fault."

**\*\*\*\*\*\*\*\*\*\***

*- Michele Hriciso, Freelance Writer/Editor*

"I was told two days before I was to go on vacation for two weeks that upon my return I would be working evening shift. (I had been working midnights.) Management told me I was chosen because I was expected to be understand-

*ing, as the person I was switching with was going to school. I was not under-standing! There were less senior people not being moved, and I had worked wherever I had been asked to work for three years without complaint. I thought seniority should count for something. I was not asked to switch shifts—I was told. This made me resentful. I had also just put in for a transfer to another unit so it made me suspicious that someone was trying to keep me from being transferred.*

*I handled it wrong. I tried going up the chain and it backfired badly, ending up with me being suspended for one day without pay for "violation of chain of command." However, I was suspended without due process—that is, I was not allowed to give a statement as to why I did what I did.*

*The whole disciplinary process was carried out while I was on vacation. The suspension paperwork also claimed it was a second offense, but I had paperwork proving the "first offense" was a simple misunderstanding and that I was never disciplined for it.*

*Two weeks after I returned to work (a month after the incident) I was sent home to serve my suspension even though the day I was supposed to serve the suspension had come and gone. I was never notified of the suspension date, and I thought it was very wrong that a date had been specified in writing but the change in the date was not specified in writing. I got a lawyer and took the problem to the appropriate unit. After an investigation was completed, the suspension was overturned. The whole process took almost six months.*

*I have no regrets about getting a lawyer. What I did was wrong, but what management did to me was worse and bordered on illegal. I could have taken a more positive attitude and gotten the shift change issue addressed in another manner."*

\*\*\*\*\*\*\*\*\*

*- Stephanie Cooks, Refund Analyst, HCA Healthcare Services:*

*"The experience I had was not having a bad attitude but dealing with people who use their position to belittle their co-workers. Having management tell you that you cannot ride to work with your co-worker or that you cannot go to lunch with your friend. Threatening you with your job or to write you up. As someone who has gone through this daily, I refuse to deal with this, and a co-worker and I took this to HR and over their heads. It was not just my friend and I, but a group of people that came together to correct the problem and due to this people lost their jobs. So make no mistake that no one has to deal with this. A corporation has no right to abuse or disrespect their employees."*

1) In reference to the above experience you just recalled, provide a concise answer to why a person should choose to have a positive attitude—that would have an end result leading to the journey of success in Corporate America.

*"A positive attitude will make your professional experience more enjoyable and rewarding and will greatly enhance your potential to be successful in your chosen field."*—**Jason Pamer, Director of Editorial at Suite101.com**

*"If one is positive one must also conduct himself in a positive way at all times. Positive thinking also results in a professional image."*—**Nathaniel Alexander, Fuel System Technician Key, Northrop Grumman Inc.**

*"I should have went to my Team Leader first and then have a three conference to discuss in detail of the matter that deeply disturbed me to work effectively."*— **Angela Stephens, Quality Analyst at Aetna US Healthcare**

*"If you get a reputation for being uncooperative, deserved or undeserved, it will eliminate your chances for promotion."—**Michele Hriciso, Freelance Writer / Editor***

*"It is best to keep a positive attitude and a clear head to deal with the situation. The outcome is helping you keep your job and not letting the manager get information that will affect your job. The outcome for me is watching my attackers get what is coming to them."—**Stephanie Cooks, Refund Analyst, HCA Healthcare Services***

2) List some ways to overcome situations that test your ability to get grounded and return your focus to the prime directive of the business entity. Limit it to four measures that you use to evaluate your issue with a co-worker, upper management, your client or customer—these measures are used to overcome anger, resentment, and jealous, that produces a negative attitude in a business environment.

*Jason Pamer, Director of Editorial at Sute101.com:*

- *Ask yourself whether the problem or conflict you're experiencing is worth your time and energy. Does it have far reaching effects on the success of your business? Are you letting personality conflicts cloud your objective thinking? It's easy to get caught up in issues that are hardly worth your valuable time and critical thought. Pick your battles wisely and don't get caught up in minor issues and problems that will deflate your enthusiasm for more important matters.*

- *Ask yourself whether you'll look back in a year and still feel that the issue or conflict you're facing is important. If the answer is no, stop letting this particular issue frustrate you or sour your attitude. Many of the problems and conflicts that create negative emotions at the workplace or between companies are "small stuff" and you'll look back and wished you focused your time and energy on more important issues.*

- *Ask yourself whether you're permitting separate or outside areas of unhappiness to cloud your vision. Are you being overly negative because you're having a bad day or something else negative is happening in your life? Try to distance outside distractions form the task at hand and don't allow negativity to creep in from outside sources.*

- *Remember that every job, position, industry has its good and bad points. You should be in your current job because you enjoy the people and the work involved. The good aspects of your current work environment, and your reason for being there, shouldn't be ruined by its less appealing traits. Remembering these facts will make the less enjoyable aspects of any job pass quickly and will allow you to focus on the parts you enjoy.*

**\*\*\*\*\*\*\*\*\***

*Nathaniel Alexander, Fuel System Technician Key, Northrop Grumman Inc.:*

- *Always have communication lines open.*
- *Be helpful.*
- *Remain confident.*
- *Be professional.*
- *Be Positive.*

**\*\*\*\*\*\*\*\*\***

*- Angela Stephens, Quality Analyst at Aetna US Healthcare:*

- *Pray to your God and ask for strength at this moment.*
- *As my longtime mate Craig always says, put it down and take a step back.*
- *Go to lunch to get away.*
- *Depending on the situation take a break.*

\*\*\*\*\*\*\*\*\*\*

*- Michele Hriciso, Freelance Writer / Editor:*

- *When someone gets negative with me, I give him or her positive right back. This gives me the upper edge, as it lets them know I will not stoop to their level. It also lets them know that I'm willing to be cooperative and work toward a resolution even if they're not.*

- *If I am wrong, I apologize. This is sometimes very hard to do, especially when you're working with someone who is manipulative. But it goes a long way toward reducing resentment; people are more likely to resent you if you take a know-it-all attitude and won't admit you're wrong.*

- *When someone is angry (and I get this a lot) I never argue with them right on the spot. I speak very calmly to them and try not to let them rattle me. If I match their anger, I can't listen to what they're saying, and I can't control the direction of the conversation. In my line of work I have to be able to direct the conversation. Most angry people just want someone to listen to them and acknowledge the validity of their problem. Doing that gives you control of the conversation and makes them much more cooperative.*

- *I don't even acknowledge jealousy anymore. It is the jealous person's problem and it only hurts me if they are lashing out at me. If they choose to go that route, eventually it backfires on them. I don't tattle on them but I do find that acting like a normal, reasonable person no matter what does a lot to defuse the effects of their jealous actions.*

**\*\*\*\*\*\*\*\*\*\***

### - Stephanie Cooks, Refund Analyst, HCA Healthcare Services

- *Talk to someone outside the situation.*
- *Maybe seek legal advice.*
- *Go to the source of the problem.*
- *Go to management or human resources.*

3) Give an example related to the incident in question 1, where if you had to do it again, what would you do or say differently?

### - Jason Pamer, Director of Editorial at Sute101.com:

*"In the above example, I would spend less time worrying about the future of the company and more time focused on the day to day work of running the company. This shift in attitude would be accomplished by remembering that the upside of working for a start-up outweighs the tough times, and that working for an established company wouldn't make me any happier. If anything, switching to an established company would be more limiting, less exciting, and would likely lead to greater frustration.*

*The tendency to fall into the "grass is greener" trap can be avoided if you con-tinually remind yourself why you've chosen the position and why you enjoy it."*

*********

*- Nathaniel Alexander, Fuel System Technician Key, Northrop Grumman Inc.:*

*"I went after my lead; if I could do it over I'll talk to my supervisor about what took place."*

*********

*- Angela Stephens, Quality Analyst at Aetna US Healthcare:*

*"I wouldn't have said anything to individual I had the issue with, rather whatever I thought of her I would have let my upper management handle it."*

*********

*- Michele Hriciso, Freelance Writer / Editor:*

*"If I had to do it again, I would have trusted my instincts and objected to the shift change in writing rather than trying to discuss it through my chain of command on the phone. At the very least you need to object to something like that in person, and it's better if it's in writing and presented in person. Otherwise you're just a faceless voice on the phone and there's no interest in you as a human being with feelings and emotions."*

*********

*- Stephanie Cooks, Refund Analyst, HCA Healthcare Services*

*"I would not change the way I solved the problem for me."*

---

4) Provide some insight on your successful measures that you took when a co-worker, colleague, upper management, client or customer had the negative/aggressive attitude limited to 5 helpful tips: Some general tips for handling negative or aggressive attitudes in the work place.

---

*- Jason Pamer, Director of Editorial at Sute101.com:*

- *Don't let someone's negativity or poor attitude dampen your enthusiasm or passion for a particular project. Remember that negative people will always see the glass as half empty, but it's still important to gather their feedback and opinions.*

- *Don't take negative attitudes personally or allow them to cause a confrontational atmosphere. Take it in stride and don't get caught up in arguing with someone about your differing attitudes.*

- *If you encounter a co-worker who's consistently negative, try infusing a more positive outlook by pointing out the positive aspects of the project or task you're working on.*

- *Believe that your positive attitude is infectious. In other words, don't hold back your enthusiasm or passion. A room full of negativity can often be overcome by one person's positive thinking.*

- *If you encounter rampant negativity and poor attitudes where you work, creating an unfulfilling and unhappy work environment, it might be time to find a new job.*

\*\*\*\*\*\*\*\*

*- Nathaniel Alexander, Fuel System Technician Key, Northrop Grumman Inc.:*

- *"Do my job and if possible do away with the middle man or lead."*

\*\*\*\*\*\*\*\*

*- Angela Stephens, Quality Analyst at Aetna US Healthcare:*

- *"Retain your positive level and keep yourself focus on the task at hand."*

- *"Come into the door stating today that this day will be a Good Day."*

- *Look at your priorities to keep a good attitude. Mine is my son to make aware that I have a child that depends on me to keep a level head so I can provide for, feed, clothed, etc.*

\*\*\*\*\*\*\*\*\*

*- Michele Hriciso, Freelance Writer / Editor:*

- *All the time people are aggressive or angry where I work. Never, ever respond to an angry person with anger. All this does is escalate the situation. Returning anger must be your last resort, when noth-ing else has worked.*

- *I have found that simple politeness works as long as it is genuine and done with respect. Being nice when you are trying to get your way is almost immediately seen as fake and disrespectful. You must respect the person behind the anger.*

- *It doesn't hurt to toss the other party a bone once in a while. Aggression and negativity often result from the person's belief that nothing ever goes their way, or that they are not being listened to or respected. Give them something small, like a sincere compliment on their clothing, or help them with a project that nobody else wants to work on. I often help people out by switching days off when they can't get vacation time and they really need a day off.*

- *Once you have shown someone respect, they are not as likely to be aggressive toward you, and perhaps it will extend to others.*

- *For years negativity has been pervasive where I work, particularly in management. In the last year it's getting better but the negativ-ity has been replaced with the management mantra "you will behave, you will cooperate"—even if it hurts you. There is no room for natural discourse or disagreement and the veneer of cooperation is easily scratched. When people have no room to disagree at all they cannot work out their conflicts in a peaceful manner and I believe this leads to aggression.*

\*\*\*\*\*\*\*\*\*

*- Stephanie Cooks, Refund Analyst, HCA Healthcare Services:*

*"My problem was with upper management and I took the problem to HR and due to that and other complaints they lost their jobs."*

**\*\*\*\*\*\*\*\*\***

5). In regards to the theme of "Your Attitude": The many years you acquire in Corporate America think of the many professional individuals that provided *wisdom* in looking at the *Big Picture*. Provide some of their advices, quotes, and as well as your own on the outlook for succeeding in Corporate America with an *awesome attitude*.

In addition, really highlight what employers say often regarding attitudes in reference to employees as well as employees say about employers / upper management.

*- Jason Pamer, Director of Editorial at Sute101.com*

*"A consistent message I've received from upper management is that a person's attitude is the most important factor when making decisions on hiring or promoting people. Everyone enjoys working with a team that includes positive thinkers who energize others. The best leaders lead by example, and a positive leader will help instill this attitude in their team.*

*My experiences hiring people and assigning projects have reflected this trend as well. I believe in rewarding your best players, and these are consistently people with good attitudes who take a positive approach to any project or challenge they take on."*

**\*\*\*\*\*\*\*\*\***

*- Nathaniel Alexander, Fuel System Technician Key, Northrop Grumman Inc.:*

*"I believe in quality not quantity."*

- *Do it right the first time.*

- *If I don't look busy, it is because I did it right the first time.*

- *Work smarter not harder.*

**\*\*\*\*\*\*\*\***

*- Angela Stephens, Quality Analyst at Aetna US Healthcare:*

*"Choose your day on how you will spend it in a positively manner. State that today will be a wonderful day."*

**\*\*\*\*\*\*\*\***

*- Michele Hriciso, Freelance Writer / Editor:*

*"In regards, to the theme of "Your Attitude": The many years you acquire in Corporate America think of the many professional individuals that provided wisdom in looking at the Big Picture. Provide some of their advices, quotes, and as well as your own on the outlook for succeeding in Corporate America with an awesome attitude. Check out the work of Zig Ziglar and Stephen*

*Covey for some great advice about success. I don't have any specific quotes at this time, but I do know that keeping a positive outlook is the most important thing you can do. If you are not open to outsiders you will be ignoring potential contacts and (even more important) the opportunity to make a true friend. You need others to succeed, and nobody wants to work with a sad sack who wears black every day and never has anything nice to say about anyone.*

*If you have the time, check out your local Toastmasters chapter. These folks can help give you invaluable career skills while you practice your public speaking skills. You learn how to conduct meetings and present yourself in a positive light, as well as making valuable contacts. Find a local club at www.toastmasters.org and get information on membership. This is by far the best way I have found to educate yourself as to how to behave in the corporate world; it costs far less than college tuition and is peer-run so your mentors are people just like you."*

\*\*\*\*\*\*\*\*

*- Stephanie Cooks, Refund Analyst, HCA Healthcare Services:*

*"The Lord will not put more on you then you can bear."*

- *Take notes and dates and times.*

- *If you can record your meetings.*

- *Keep the questions to the point.*

- *Do not sign documents that you feel uncomfortable with.*

\*\*\*\*\*\*\*

**In conclusion:**

<u>An Exercise For You:</u>

Answer these questions:

- Write down what the term "team player" means to you. Don't judge your thoughts; let them flow instantly.

- What measure of activity motivates you to focus on the job task at hand?

- What are you looking for in your direct supervisor to influence your interests, determination, and dedication to your job and to a particular project?

- For the management level, what are you looking for in the people that work for you to influence your interests, determination, and dedication to continue to be an effective and compassionate leader, in order to get task done?

- Do you volunteer to help your co-workers to successfully accomplish the company goals?

- Do you present confidence, calmness, and a strong focus on the initiative?

- Do you look at the big picture of getting to the destination mapped out by the company, and listen to both sides of the argument at hand?

<u>Read over your answers and see how it relates to the below definition of a team:</u>

**<u>Team</u>:** A *cooperative* effort by a group of persons acting together as one entity to accomplish a set goal.

The key word in this definition is cooperative where the term is most often used by an employer when looking for a new hire—a team *player* to join our company.

The questions I posed were geared to stimulate your way of thinking towards awareness of having and sustaining a good attitude. Your attitude affects the way others perceive you and your feelings towards a job task. If you are angry with a co-worker or manager, you will most definitely not volunteer to do the extra tasks needed to complete a project. And most of the time the reason for your state is personal. If you let this anger grow deeper in your heart, you will become unapproachable and your reputation as being cooperative will be ruined. If you choose to think only of an individual, not as a team, your journey will not be a successful one.

Yes, there are incidents when you must take a stand to point the team in another direction. But it must be done in a professional way and at the proper time; these measures will be outline later on in the book. Your primary goal here is making sure your foundation is purged of negative thoughts and personal issues that will block your vision of being a team player in Corporate America: surviving your journey towards success by accomplishing your goals.

# CHAPTER 2

# Your Career Goals And Your Passion

Once you have the ability to define your goals within the corporate framework, you can make your journey towards success a meaningful one for you and others on the same course.

The next area of focus you will need to look at and accomplish in gearing your compass towards success are your career goals and your passion. Why the two? Simple. These two areas of focus will allow you to stay on course of your journey as well as determine to you when you need to take that *right* or *left* turn…or for most…*full steam ahead*. Also, when you know that you are in your right career, then you are living your passion. Living your passion will enable you to reinforce your great attitude. You will be pure and sincere when you approach others and feel good about what you are performing on a daily basis: while enjoying your journey.

Oftentimes we ignore the hidden passions of our hearts, and we choose to go down the wrong career path. This chapter will outline some pivotal steps to help you get closer to your career goals and your true passion in order to sustain your great attitude. Remember, having a great attitude in Corporate America is crucial and keeping this spirit relates to the following questions: *"Are you satisfied with your job? Are you happy with what you are doing?"*

If the answer is no or maybe, then you need to regroup. If you say yes, then a review of your career focus won't deter you from your chosen path, but rather will keep you on course.

First, you need to review your life as a whole and think of the things you enjoyed at different companies you worked at. Try to recall a particular task that you might think was insignificant and the jobs that required a lot of responsibility. Ask yourself what is most important to you now and what will be most important to you in the future. Did any of the previous and current job tasks you performed interest you enough to keep you headed in that direction or did it encourage you to try something new?

Here are some exercises to help you come closer to realizing your career goals and your true passion:

### Exercise One:

On a piece of paper to the left make a dot and to the far right make another dot. Draw a straight line from the dot on the left side and connect it to the dot on the right side. The dot on the left represents where you were first starting off in Corporate America. The middle symbolizes where you are now and the far right symbolizes where you wish to be in your career. Some of you might be just starting off and may be to the far left, and others might be in the middle still, and then there might be those that are near retirement or others that are still in their chosen field. No matter where you are, this exercise will still be helpful for you to review your life to make choices allowing you to stay on course.

Draw a circle on the straight line at the point where you feel you are in your career right now. This circle represents the current path you are taking in Corporate America. Now observe what you are doing now in your current career. Ask yourself honestly if you are content with what you are doing. Do not put off what needs to be examined. Stop saying: *"I am just too busy to answer that call to change your career."* and decide to answer that call. We all at times need to review the course of our lives in order to make necessary adjustments and changes to our charted course.

To help you visualize your career path and to proceed forward, you will have to answer some questions that will lead you either forward, standstill, or backward to nowhere.

Ask yourself these questions: Note: a space is an inch.

1. Are you happy doing the job tasks that you are currently doing? If yes move forward two spaces.

2. Is your current industry the one you dreamed of and would continue to feel comfortable with in the near future? If yes move forward three spaces.

3. Have you spent ample time learning new technology techniques in the chosen industry you are in? If yes move forward two spaces.

4. Do you look forward to the next business day to tackle the new stack of work waiting for you or the one you left behind because it pleases you? If yes move forward three spaces.

5. Have you indicated to your management your interest in things that will further your career? If yes move forward four spaces.

6. Did you enroll in any corporate sponsored seminars emphasizing team building skills, in order to make you a better candidate for new positions that match your career goals? If yes move forward three spaces.

7. Have you taken the *"wait and see"* attitude—waiting to see what your colleagues will do before you move into action? Stay where you are.

8. Do you feel that what you are doing is good enough, fine enough, and you don't volunteer for anything due to the fear of responsibility? If yes move back four spaces.

9. Do you continuously keep a good rapport with other employees who might one day be your allies in leading you to your chosen career path? If yes move forward seven spaces.

10. Are you excited when your ideas are accepted and implemented? Do you eagerly participate in matters that showcase your best talents? If yes move forward three spaces.

Take a look at your progress. Observe where you are and where you feel you need to be. Listening to your inner voice will always steer you in the right direction—even if it tells you to no longer work for a major corporation, but rather to open up a flower shop. The key is to understand your true purpose in life and where you need to make the next turn on your journey.

Understanding that you must know your career goals and the steps you are currently making—either getting you there or getting you nowhere will help you achieve a successful journey in Corporate America.

Being in an environment that is a challenge, fulfilling, and rewarding to yourself will allow you to function positively. Your passion is the brother/sister to your career goals because it allows you to sustain a balance of happiness, doing what job task you are performing no matter what level of an employee you are. Honoring your true passions will in turn keep your attitude in an expression that is fulfilling to yourself as well as to your co-workers because you are where you want to be—*and you love your job*.

## Career Counselors

When you are on the verge of changing your career, you might want to use a career counselor. Career counselors can find your desired career and assist in identifying individual core skills and competencies. In addition, they can assist in researching different career fields and discovering great possibilities. Creating networking skills in which are extremely important when you are seeking a new line of work. When working with a career counselor, you should realize that it usually takes more than 1 or 2 sessions, depending on how extensively you want to use their services.

Here is a brief list of other services career counselors can offer:

- Administer tests to assess skills, abilities, and interests to identify career options.

- Introducing or training on new skills to update your knowledge in other technical areas.

- Improve the client decision-making skills.

- Coach the client in job-hunting strategies and skills.

- Assist in the development of resumes.

- Help prep the client on interviewing so the client can communicate effectively.

- Negotiate job offers, raises, and promotions successfully.

- Help the client determine whether the best career option is to start his or her own business.

- Negotiate a favorable severance or buyout package if you're downsized.


**Finding a Career Counselor**

Having a career counselor should be done very carefully as you will be working closely with this individual. Always make sure the counselor has the proper background, education and credentials that will guarantee you a great result in the search process of a new career. Research the career counselor with the National Board for Certified Counselors (www.nbcc.org/) where you can find a list of certified counselors in your state. The "National Certified Career Counselor" designation indicates that the career counselor has achieved the highest certification in a particular profession.

A Certified Career Counselor will mean that the professional have earned a graduate degree in related professional field and/or counseling from a respected accredited institution. Your chosen career counselor will have also completed supervised counseling experience which included a minimum of two years of full-time career development work experience in a specified career counseling.

When you decide on a career counselor you both should have a solid understanding of expectations, services provided, and any additional fees. Make sure you are given an itemized list listing time commitments, a detailed explanation of services, and a copy of the code of ethics.

**Your Rights**

A certified career counselor will always respect your certain rights and present your best interests in the search for a better career opportunity.

Below are a few known consumer rights:

Personal data and your qualifications should always be kept between you and your counselor including all communication to is to be treated confidentially—and get a copy the code of ethics to which your counselor adheres.

Contacts and phone numbers are shared between you and your counselor assure that you have the first dibs to opportunities that do arise.

~ ~ ~

You can also help the outcome of your job search by reading and participating in job boards that provide a full range of different professionals discussing their current industry in and outs. Another good idea is joining an industry association—this will provide you much information, networking opportunities, and first hand experience in the field you are curious about. Contact your mentor or someone that you truly look up to in order to get feedback on staying on track. Listen. Take notes and monitor your progress. Choose wisely and stay on course!

PART TWO

# WORKING WITH DIFFER-
# ENT PERSONALITIES

# CHAPTER 3

# Effective Verbal & Written Communication

Nichel Anderson:

*"I stated my answer like a moving automotive, and before I knew it the well tailored man across from me quickly wrote down my response. I needed this job, and I could tell the interviewer needed to fill it just the same but was hesitant. My mind raced for the right words to say and then I was suddenly inspired. I slowly and effectively asked about the new software that was out that has been reported to do wonders with crunching data in a productive environment. I continue to demonstrate my knowledge and recent experience of the new technology in a clear and concise manner...His eyes lifted up with intense interest and a sparkle of light...I ended up getting the job."*

## Effective Verbal Communication

The above episode demonstrates the effectiveness of verbal communication. On most employers' job requirements in searching for new employees, this is one area of expertise that is always required. Why is this? Quite simple. It displays your ability to communicate the company's objective clearly and concisely to their customers or clients. This is crucial to the success of any company that aspires to reach their set goals and beat their competitors. Most of us take this for granted and do not try to hone on our vocabulary, speech pathology, and pronunciation. Mastering effective verbal communication will also assist you greatly when you want to accomplish your own professional goals, like in the episode I just presented, and perhaps during a corporate catch 20-20 situation.

Surviving in Corporate America can be tricky and very challenging because it relies on so many vitally important areas you are responsible for, i.e. your mortgage, rent, car, child care, and a comfortable way of life. You see the power of the entity that you work for or about to enter into the corporate environment, a person must master the area of respecting the territory of Corporate America profound power. Speaking with a solid foundation and a clear mission to your objective in this type of environment of structure and position is very crucial. Adapting to the ability to know when and what type of approach to use with individuals in management or a same level co-worker is crucial as well.

What are the techniques to mastering effective verbal communication? Lets begin with an exercise and some episodes.

First, how is your vocabulary? Is it bland or is it non-corporate talk? Begin to implement the following measures in overcoming this obstacle:

- Those long in-depth Corporate memos from the CEO, COO, CFO, Owner, etc., that you usually press delete and forget about it, instead, print it out and get a highlighter and pen. Begin to read the memo and start circling the words that you do not know the meaning of and the ones that you usually do not use in your everyday vocabulary.

- Look up the words that you do not know the meaning of and start developing ways to use them in a complete sentence.

- Another option is being alert to listening to upper management who speaks in a meeting. Observe the words the manager is using and watch out for a particular word that the manager always uses. One particular divisional manager, I worked for used the word integrity all the time. When I started to implement the word in my verbal communication to other business entities, I saw a more trusted look and understanding of the delivery of my message across their faces.

~ ~ ~

Now you have an idea on how to expand your vocabulary, but how do you effectively deliver it? Well, you first have to find out what type of speaker you are so you can successfully reach your goal in speaking effectively. Most of us are either:

1. Motor mouth (Speak fast)

2. Washer Machine mouth (Speak fast and slur or combine words together)

3. Stutter Mouth

4. Low Voice

5. High Voice

6. Unbalance volume tone voice

7. Trailer Mouth (Start at right volume then trail off to no-man's land)

**Effective Ways of Speaking:**

There is a way to overcome these areas of bad speaking. It relies on one word:

*Concentration.* It is truly that easy. Knowing first what you intend to say and to concentrate on the choice words coming out of your mouth. Breathe in and out to keep a rhythm of what you are delivering. When you speak, say each word as if the word is standing alone and deserves the respect to be delivered in its own unique way.

For example, say the sentence below out loud and concentrate on each word. Pay attention to your speed and your pronunciation by making sure you are hitting your t's, d's, and k's:

*"I went to Susie and asked her where the file was. She stated that Billy carried the file to Roth's desk."*

A very good practice to master is learning to think before you speak. I often try to order my thoughts that I wish to convey to others at meetings. I present my forthcoming statement in the following order:

1. The main cause of the problem that would prevent the job task initiative, I would present in one sentence the direct objective.

2. Under the main cause, I would provide examples of what I am referring to.

3. In addition, I would present any other issues that either relates to the first one presented or additional issues that would cause problems in getting the job done.

4. Next, I would state any questions that I might have to further understanding the implementations of doing the tasks; I would ask direct questions and do not prolong my query.

5. I would also make a point to some of the instructions—reasons why the new procedures are in place, and other measures outlined to showcase I have a fundamental knowledge of the job task at hand but need further guidance. This would demonstrate to the lead or supervisor you are very interested in the initiative and that you are a team player in hoping for a successful result.

6. I would also word my questions that it would provide answers to seeing the initiative in concrete terms. This is important because most of the time the answers that you get can be told in random terms and you are jotting down as fast as you can to keep up. Listen to the answers being presented and jot down each relevance point being instructed.

7. Afterwards be prepared to ask the lead or supervisor to repeat his/her answer in order for you to confirm that you fully understand completely.

8. You should always demonstrate courtesy to others who cut in and ask their questions because they want further understanding as well. A good team player will listen to his/hers peers and most of the time learns from his/hers peers queries.

9. Once you have another chance to continue with your questions, you should proceed and continue to jot down the answers that are presented. Remember to always be patient even if the lead or supervisor might not

have the answer and will have to get back with you. That is ok. The point is to present the questions for management to be aware that full understanding is met with the team in order to meet the team's initiative.

10. Finally, you should recap what you have learned from your questions by repeating what you learned. State from the beginning of doing the job task and present different scenarios that may come up and how to solve them based on what management instructed the team to do. Then you should end with the final step or outcome for resolution. This method will increase your knowledge of the job task and reinforce to management that they have effectively presented effective verbal communication.

~ ~ ~

Are you speaking with good grammar? This is also very crucial. Most of us don't listen to what we are saying; rather, we speak sometimes how we often write a note—fast and not using the spelling and grammar function on our word processor. But this ability to listen and make sure you are in verb agreement is crucial.

Let's do an exercise:

*"Bill ain't in no condition to work on Jones' case."*

Does this sentence sound correct? It doesn't, but trust me, most employees speak this way without realizing that is incorrect speaking in a professional environment. The following sentence is how it should have been spoken:

*"Bill is in no condition to work on Mr. Jones' case."*

Lets look at another exercise:

*"All of the patients' accounts is under recalculation to compute what the correct reimbursements need to be done, with the hope the new procedure tallies everything."*

Now in this example a couple of things are occurring. First, the verb agreement needs to be corrected, and second a new wording needs to be presented more clearly and professional. It should read:

*"All of the patients' accounts are recalculated to compute what the correct reimbursements needed in order to be allocated successfully."*

Remember to always use a singular verb with a singular subject and a plural verb when the subject is plural. Always capture the talent to listen well and then respond with calm resolve by speaking slowly in order to deliver your message effectively.

Lets do an episode exercise to mastering effective verbal communication:

**Episode 1:**

Janet, the divisional manager of Itech Inc., was very upset the cost report did not show the last quarter figures. Susan is responsible for updating the cost report and is on the phone when Janet approaches. Identify which one is not using effective verbal communication:

*"Are you about to deliver the updated cost figures?" Janet asked.*

*"Susan placed her hand on the phone receiver. "I am in the process to send the actual figures right now."*

*"Well, you coulda sent me an email of your lateness." Janet turned abruptly and headed to her office.*

~ ~ ~

There are a lot of areas that need correcting, but it will be brought up in a future chapter. For now, Janet is the culprit who is not using effective verbal communication. She should have said:

*"Susan do you have the current updated figures?"*

And then:

*"Well, you should have sent me an email stating the delayed reporting."*

The objective here is being direct in the actual issue and at the same time query for a solution or reasoning. Speaking with the correct word usage and grammar will project a more assertive, confident, and professional impression. In Corporate America, an employee and employer need to project their delivery effectively to reach desired results.

Some helpful suggestions to improve your delivery to other people are by practicing in front of others. Set a special place and time with those you trust to give you a more constructive feedback by speaking on any topic for 2 or 3 minutes. Learn to listen to your audience's responses and try to hear the objectives and points that are presented for you to reply effectively.

Begin taking notes of the constructive criticism you receive and the positive responses as well. Read over your notes and make a mental note to yourself to work on the areas that need focus and more practice. Keep your practice times at least 15 minutes a session. Also, make plans to spread out your practice session to about 3 to 4 times a week in order to keep the repetitive measures fresh in your mind.

Lastly, think about investing in a mini tape recorder. This is an excellent way to hear yourself speak and be your own judge. You can count on your successful delivery of speech when your audience move from 4 people on your team to 100 in corporate functions or events. And you will succeed in having effective verbal communication.

~ ~ ~

**Effective Written Communication**

Wherever you go to work in Corporate America, you can rest assure that written communication will be the main integral part of your job. Mastering this area of expertise will surely place you in the forefront of an effective player in Corporate America. At times, we can get overshadowed and miss the perfect opportunity to expose our intellect, passion for our job, and commitment to excellence. Writing is a powerful tool, and once you become accustomed to the types of writing styles, you should have complete understanding, and you should implement the lessons you learned here into your everyday job activities to achieve success in the journey.

I know some of us are not writers foremost, but we do know what the issue is at hand and what needs to be done to resolve the problem. Now, there are also times when we don't have a solution but still need to present the issue in order to receive a future answer. These scenarios are most common in the work environment today. However, I will present other scenarios where you have to write a rebuttal or a follow-up. Let us first start with an issue that needs a quick resolution:

**Episode 1:**

Jackie Smith is the manager for Haweson Billing Services, Inc.; she just received a fax from a provider requesting an analysis for the low revenue of return for last month totals. Jackie is new to the company and she is not familiar with the database to assist this client. Her immediate Supervisor is out of the office till Friday, so the other manager in charge in the department is Troy Johnson. Jackie did indicate to the provider that she called him back upon faxing out the requested document. Biting her nails, Jackie is so nervous as she fumbles from screen to screen to get the requested data. It has been four months since she started and she feels the pressure of not quite knowing where to maneuver throughout the company's mainframe computer. So, Jackie decides to email Troy for assistance and below is her first note:

*DEAR TROY,*

*I REALLY NEED YOUR HELP PLEASE STOP BY MY OFFICE IN A HURRY. I DON'T KNOW WHAT I AM DOING PLAYING AROUND IN THESE MANY DATABASES. PLEASE HELP!!!*

*JACKIE SMITH*
*ACCOUNTING MANAGER*
*ROTESH INC.*

I assumed you have guessed the first error Jackie made. Her first flaw was that she used all caps and this screams un-professionalism immediately. Secondly, she used sentences that do not place her at the highest light of competence to management and this is another big no-no. You never want to talk bad about yourself, trust me; the cutthroat individuals

Corporate America will have plenty to shovel dirt on you. In addition to why this is crucial is that if you are in a management position, you are the leader and these tid bits of professionalism and effective written communication should have been learned way before you stepped into this level of responsibility and position.

When you are in this type of scenario, you want to provide just enough information to the recipient, and you want to be short and always sweet when asking for help. Trust me you will get fast results. Now, below is what I recommend Jackie should have written:

*Dear Troy,*

*I am so sorry to bother you because I know you very busy this morning. I your assistance to help me locate the data containing Dr. Holmes' analysis totals for last month. He just called me and was very upset that the totals did not match what the hard copy print-out states that his office received at month-end.*

*Anytime today would be so much appreciated for I promised Dr. Holmes that I would provide him with the requested data no later than the end of this business day.*

*Again, I do apologize for any inconvenience this may have caused.*

*Thank you in advance,*
*Jackie Smith*
*Accounting Manager*
*Rotesh Inc.*

~ ~ ~

You see the key is to keep it short but sweet, and in the note provide enough to present the problem and how you intend to solve it, which in this case additional assistance is needed to handle a very urgent matter. And acknowledge that you are taking them away from their job activities and that you are very sorry for any inconvenience it may cause—this is a sure way to get a positive response and assistance right away.

Now let us look at another scenario and one of my most challenging ones as well as rewarding. Always remember, *the pen is mightier than the sword.* This brings us to writing a rebuttal to whomever is causing a conflict of interest to you that will affect your personal file with the company. Below is a great example of what I am referring to.

Lets have a look:

**Episode 2:**

Barbara Wells sat patiently while her immediate supervisor went over her yearly review. She kept eye contact and shuffled in her seat when comments were made by her supervisor of her performance. When the supervisor was finished, the supervisor asked if there was anything Barbara would like to say or add to the document. Barbara calmly commented of her disagreement of the review and kept her defense brief and to the point. In addition, Barbara indicated to her supervisor that she would rather respond by writing up her response/rebuttal and attach the word document as such. The supervisor nodded, and Barbara managed to get up and leave the conference room with a calm facial expression. However, Barbara was livid as she made it to her desk but quickly took ten deep breaths to her get thoughts together. When she was somewhat calm she went to Microsoft Word on her PC and began to type:

*Attn:*
*Curtis Banders*
*Manager for Scientific Research Dept.*

*John Rowe*
*Human Resources Manager*
*In response to the review the following was written:*

*I appreciate the opportunity of expanding my professional horizon in Biotech Scientific Research Department, and it is so fulfilling to feel more comfortable in doing my job as a researcher. I am motivated to do my part in meeting our team goals, in which, the Biotech Division will then be able to accomplish Corporate set initiatives.*

*In response, to the additional feedback relating to contributing positively at meetings, I feel it should be viewed in context of the situation. If my different approach is just that different in achieving the goals of the unit, it is not to imply that no respect was to the moderator's agenda—meaning gestures, if said occurred, could be taken or interpreted the wrong way. I always offer, and will continue to do so, helpful suggestions to make the unit the very best that it can be. As I did with my manager on a one on one pre-90 day review back in August, concerning the unit's work flow. Furthermore, I feel that all communication is important both verbally and physically, and I know that I have not interrupted, challenged, or interrogated management, rather provided enough ideas and suggestions to make the Biotech Division the very best it can be.*

*I would like to ask since incidents can be difficult to label as derogatory or not—that management request an one on one confidential meeting so we could discuss in detail. I strongly believe this measure of action will resolve any future miscommunication and prevent un-necessary and derogatory discussions of the issue in front of the team unit.*

*I value the opportunity that I was given to be a part of the Biotech Scientific Laboratory area, and I am eagerly anticipating many professional challenging goals. In addition, I look forward to meeting and exceeding the company business initiatives for corporate.*

*Sincerely.*

*Barbara Wells*

~ ~ ~

You can tell that the review was somewhat geared towards several negative performance evaluations from working as a team; an incident that the supervisor viewed the occurrence in the wrong way, and a notation of a possible uncertainty with future career goals. Barbara handled each negative remark excellently. She was professional in her response to her supervisor's review because she was not in the attack mode. Barbara defended her position, but she was doing it effectively by using appropriate words. That was the key.

**Being Empowered To Writing Effectively**

Implement the following mental note when you are placed in this kind of situation to defend yourself in Corporate America. Remember, most of your correspondence especially your performance review will be in your personal file allowing any future management personal to view the documents within. It would be hard to explain your anger and position because you might not even get an internal interview when you are trying to post out the department you are currently in.

1. Always start off your letter in a positive and great attitude. This will set your tone of professionalism and present no hint on your end that it is personal issues between you and your supervisor. Begin your complete review of the thrilling feeling of getting through the recent months at the company. Continue to indicate in the first paragraph that the experience was such a challenge to reach this point in your career.

2. The middle paragraph should start into the areas that were a criticism towards your performance that you are in a disagreement. Don't say, "that my supervisor is telling a lie on so and so or my supervisor have told an untruth. Instead write your letter in a way that you are presenting your response to the comments made about you. Do not use your supervisor name; instead, refer to management when you are talking about your direct lead person.

3. Keep each of your responses short. Use Word to pre-write your responses. Keep them 1 to 2 sentences per response.

4. If you have any dates of specific meetings with management or one and one conference session present them in your response.

5. Also, include any final agreement you had between you and your manager about implementing improvement. It will continue to show your effort for improvement and your focus on your job performance.

6. In the last paragraph, begin with where you see yourself at the company. Continue to keep a determined and upbeat attitude. Remember, your tone in your letter depicts your attitude and that is everything in Corporate America.

7. Lastly, end with a powerful sentence either at the end of the last paragraph or a separate sentence describing in a nutshell—that throughout all

the challenges your prime objective is growing with the company and meeting the business initiatives. It is a great way to show your manager and human resources manager that you are a team player and are determined to succeed.

~ ~ ~

Lets assume a conflict is between you and a fellow co-worker/colleague and you wish to settle the dispute. The point to remember is that you wish to present your side in a non-constricted way in order for your side to be heard. In addition, the letter you write should pose a response on safe terms in order to resolve or clear up any issues so that future working relations can continue. Try the bottom approach:

*Terrance,*

*I was concerned with your comment yesterday concerning the Robertson's file—that we (the team) don't have to put up with Janet for the length of the special project do we? I wish not to be a bother and regret that I ever asked take over the Robertson's file. I also would like to add that it is not because of the size and high publicity of the file that I wish to take it on by myself. I have countless experience in the field that is tailored to the magnitude of what the Robertson's file requires and professionally felt I would the perfect candidate.*

*However, if you wish to be assigned the Robertson's file then by all means I will step aside, and I am sorry for any inconvenience I may have caused. I will refrain from placing any leniency on me due to my short addition to your team from Corporate Headquarters to assist your department. That was not my true intention, and I wish not for anyone to have to put up with me during my short time here at this office site.*

*Again, I regret for any inconvenience this may have caused.*

*Sincerely,*
*Janet Rice*
*B.C. Technologies Expert*

~ ~ ~

Using the techniques in these types of scenarios will surely place you in the minds that can advance your career. You have shown that you can rise above adversity and keep your focus on the corporate business agendas.

You should also know when to carbon copy other individuals on the notes you send when an issue arrives. Follow the methods below to know when you implement this:

A. In the episode I previously presented regarding your performance review, your manager and HR need to be on the email and have a copy of the letter.

B. If the issue is between you and your manager on a particular job issue that you are responsible for, then only address your manager. However, when someone else has their hands in the pot and plays an integral part in the result that is causing your manager to question you, then you need to mention him/her as well and carbon copy.

C. When you have an on going problem with HR that still has not been fixed, then you need to send a carbon copy to your manager, the contact person you have been talking to resolve the issue, and any HR manager on your follow-up note. Trust me, once the contact person sees management is getting informed you will get results. But, you should be very discrete in your follow-up note. Do not blame or show any anger of the ongoing unresolved issue.

D. In the incident when your co-worker refuses to correct a mistake on a case, and you have continually sent a request. On your next note, you should carbon copy your immediate supervisor and send another note.

~ ~ ~

### Example of Contributing Suggestions For The Company

There are many other scenarios that come your way in Corporate America that you must respond by writing. But lets say that you are called upon to present ideas to better help the team or division. I know one area that is always requested by employees to provide feedback and that is in the area of training. Many of times not sufficient and effective training programs in Corporate America succeed in training employees, rather the training area will then need a more focused approach. Below is an example of how you can present your ideas professionally in solving the un-effectiveness of the company-training program:

### Suggestions:

I feel that our training needs improving in two areas, for example, the orientation and on the job training:

### Orientation:

There should be a much better way of exposure to new employees of the *Welcome Criteria;* for example, the presenting a positive attitude towards team-work, the importance of confidentiality, the benefits package, the office site tour, etc.

I suggest perhaps have two days of exposure to the above mention focus. This way we can get all the necessary HR and other general questions out of the way that did not get covered at the interview process.

The remaining days should be focused on preparing for OJT: On the job training. In addition, the contents of the training should cover the core specifics of job. The additional assistance once the employee reach the department to work.

From the third day to the remaining company set training days, employees should be exposed to all of the sub-systems—along with exercises that will gain employees the knowledge to gather information from that system.

Note: *A sufficient time should be spent on each one with tests for employees and the copies of the graded tests should be given to employees.*

Results: Will provide the employees must less anxiety of not knowing where to go to do their particular job.

**On The Job Training:**

There should be a Buddy System:

The Work Buddy is the development coach and the person that is very knowledgeable, approachable, and is excellent in communicating the core specifics of the job at hand:

During this introduction, the Work Buddy should go over the below objectives to allow the new employee to perform his/her daily routine.

1. A tour needs to be done, meeting the team, focusing on the necessary contact people the employees might need in order to accomplish their job, and forward work to.

2. A print out sheet listing the step-by-step responsibilities from beginning to end what that particular position does each day.

3. The new employee should also have all necessary forms, links, etc.

4. The new employee should have specific time spent with their Work Buddy—and should be going over the step-by-step sheet and working accounts—the first two days.

**A Work Buddy System:**

a. The Work Buddy should designate another well-trained co-worker in the next cubicle to the new employee—so the new employee can ask any urgent questions that may arise.

b. The Work Buddy should have a time schedule to sit with the new employee where the Work Buddy focus is on effectively training the new employee.

c. This schedule for one on one focus should be 2 hours in order to give every employee full advantage of the Work Buddy knowledge.

**Added suggestions:**

There should also be weekly meetings, for a month, with new employees and the Work Buddies and Management to provide honest feedback of the new employees progress. Then perhaps combine the team so the new employees will not get confused with older employees more advanced knowledge on the job duties.

~ ~ ~

Keep in mind to present your ideas chronologically. Start with the most important areas that need to be focused on and end with the final area that must be reviewed and accomplished. Use concise words that are to the point and easy to interpret your ideas.

Finally, in writing effectively in any mode of response or presentation remember to be professional. In Corporate America, there are many times when you are in a difficult situation, however, mastering on how to write to accomplish the desired results is the key to writing effectively.

# CHAPTER 4

# Developing and Sustaining Good Interpersonal Skills

Rita Lowes, a director of a major real estate company:

*"Yes, I feel that the Hamilton file needs to be incorporated with the redone restate calculation and profile so we can better initiate our success, Ann, you are such an asset for working overtime with me and accomplishing our goals." Rita Lowes said before hanging up the conference call."*

*Three days later, Rita sent Ann a cookie bouquet with a card: You are one in a million, thanks again a whole sweet bunch."*

Often times we forget that the little small gestures go a long way. We tend to feel we are just there for our bills to get paid, when in fact we are there without even knowing it, making relationships, and enriching our interpersonal skills. Therefore, we as success bound individuals must realize to have a solid bridge with other co-workers, colleagues and management of any business sector. During our hours spent at work, we forget the most important factor we are engaged in: working with others. There are so many different personalities that you will or are already in contact with during your daily work day. In succeeding in Corporate America, no matter what level you are on the career ladder, you must master this area of focus.

Yes, your attitude is number one in your journey to success, but while you are have a great attitude, there can be those individuals with a personality that try to bring you down and send you backwards rather than forward. You must begin to realize the significance in the many personalities in the corporate environment—and how you must hold onto your own self-resilience in order to overcome the many and challenging obstacles in getting along or learning to work effectively with others. Our everyday lives within Corporate America challenges us to either succeed or fail; I learn that we must use methods to help us stay on course. The many methods used could be either poems or passages that provides encouragement. Throughout this chapter I will provide inserts that often uplifts my spirit on my journey towards success.

I have posed a few questions to a very effective team player and a guru of great interpersonal skills with team members and upper management; Katie Howald, a Medicare Coordinator at West Florida Regional Medical Center.

**An Interview With A Golden Team Player:**

*Nichel:*

What do you feel your personality needs to project in order to sustain good interpersonal skills with co-workers?

*Katie:*

You should have understanding and always treat each person as an individual and as you would like to be treated. Listen and don't judge. Do not join cliques and take sides. Instead work as a team!

*Nichel:*

What are the key things you make sure that you say or do to keep good feelings between co-workers?

*Katie:*

Do not criticize. Instead respect each other's opinions. Know that you are not always right. Lend a helping hand. Smile and go on your way. Do not point fingers example; she/he did not do this, etc.

~ ~ ~

### Keeping good relations with co-workers in Corporate America:

Having good interpersonal relations with others in Corporate America is the most critical measure of success. In most cases, individuals with power miss this class and focus on power rather than sustaining good interpersonal skills. What does this lead to when the class is missed? A team or organization that is not unified to the company's initiative, instead, the company has a high turnover rate of employees. The communication line is broken due to the inability to communicate to employees effectively by empowering the workforce—instead of creating a hostile and resentful environment due to poor interpersonal skills.

The old rule of treating others the way we want to be treated is the way to go. The only difference when the individual is in a managerial position—is that—there must be a strong ability to know when to be firm and when not to be firm in order to keep the line of good interpersonal relationship in force rather than broken. At times the energy of power can blind those to a point that they lose ground with their employees, and the department suffers greatly with low morale, and employees transferring out of the area or leaving the company completely. To achieve success in this area, one needs to know how to effectively motivate the Company/Division/Team successfully. In addition, I would cover the true characteristic of an effective CEO/Manager/Team Leader as well as the effectiveness of words.

**Mastering Great Interpersonal Skills:**

Lets begin reviewing what we must master in achieving great interpersonal skills:

- Motivating your Company/Division/Team successfully.
- The Perils of Favoritism.
- True characteristic of an effective CEO/Manager/ Team Leader.

**Motivating your Company/Division/Team:**

*Respect*—Honor others' feelings, as well as, yours to assure a good working relationship. Ask yourself; *Would I like to be treated or talked too that way?* Conduct an one/one conference to resolve a problem or issue but never in front of other team members to boost your ego when really all it does destroys a working relationship with your employee.

*Honest*—Tell the truth and admit when you are wrong even if you might be responsible for a portion of the problem. This will release the tendency to blame others and not being able to own up to responsibility.

*Trustworthy*—Keep your word. Stand up for your unit to gain continued support and a devoted team that will have your back when you need it the most.

*Fair*—Treat all equally. Don't show favoritism. We are human and tend to really like someone better than others. However, the platform of being in a position that has power to manage others, you will need to regulate attention, special projects, and occurring assignments to equally give each employee a fair chance to spread their creativity.

*Creative*—Show you care by surprising your employees or fellow colleagues by giving them some candy, or a special paid luncheon, or a thank you note.

*Mastering these areas of focus will 100% guarantee a motivated team to work well with you as well as with fellow team members.

**The Perils OF Favoritism**

A person with power and a title to match can often become a balancing act in motivating a team to reach the company's main initiative. Most of the time the manager or team leader seem to admire or appreciate an employee or a couple of employees more than the rest of the team. *"How to steer away from this path?"… "What should the employees who are not the chosen ones overcome the effects of the perils of favoritism?"*

**On the management level implement the following:**

> a. Always demonstrate honesty when assessing your decisions to pick a particular employee…is the right person for the assignment.

b. Listen to others who come to you with concern towards your consistent selection of a particular employee.

c. Take time to observe all of your team members and assess their strengths and weakness. Also, you should over time see how they improve in the weaker areas.

d. Even when you come back to the same person for the assignment, in which, this assessment will be difficult to prove to your team that you that favors favoritism. Try instead to pick someone other than your usual selection by providing an opportunity to prove to yourself as well as to the team—that a different employee can succeed at the task at hand. You really don't know how someone different from your usual selection will perform until you give another person a chance.

**The effects of favoritism on the employee level should do the following:**

a. When you are on the outside looking in can be difficult to handle, instead of being mad and having a bad attitude, an employee should write down experiences that prove favoritism is being orchestrated in the department.

b. Provide enough solutions how you feel that will remedy the situation to bring fairness in the team. Stay away from personal thoughts by only leaving professional feedback.

c. Request a confidential meeting with management and present your issue along with your suggested solutions to fix the problem.

d. Be very direct with your statements but have your tone pleasant. This measure will insure to management you wish to work as a team, and that everyone should be valued of what they contribute to the team—not just one particular individual or a selected few.

By making an honest effect to being fair when selecting those best for the job, a manager should always apply the requirements to the right candidate. As a team at whole, diversity is the key to remember by picking different people to do an assignment. Your team in return will respect you as a fair, caring, and professional manager.

## An Effective CEO / Manager / Team Lead:

*Respect*—Value your employees, and you will gain ultimate respect towards you personally and your position within the company. Respect diversity from religious holidays, culture preferences to the unique creativity that diversity brings to the table.

*Patience*—Be willing to wait for your employees to demonstrate effective managing of their assigned duties. For example, you should consider allowing an allotted time for improvement and an opportunity to gain respect that you are a fair person.

*Honest*—Understanding that the truth gains a strong relationship with your team, and you will be considered one of the few approachable and honest managers to work for. Telling the truth can be tricky when times are stressful and uncertainty is present, but being honest to your employees that soon more information will be presented is the best choice to make.

*Experience*—Know your job and company's main purpose and mission to accomplishing the initiatives. Stop depending on your employees to carry you. Instead, you lead the team by carrying your own weight...and the team will follow with certainty.

*Writing Communication Effectively*—Always present a sense of approachness during non-tension times or during high-tension times, you should write to encourage togetherness not division. Never write angry or hostile words in order to get your team doing as you see fit because it will always back fire. Choose your words wisely.

*Verbal Communication Effectively*—Speak with care and give eye contact. Only emphasize your message with your hands when appropriately but keep it to a medium. You want your team to focus on you and what you are saying that will affect them as a whole. Listen intently and answer the question directly without going off topic.

~ ~ ~

Words can be a powerful method to demonstrate ones thought and purpose; an individual with power to manage others should always use caution in the words they use. The ability to choose wisely of the words spoken, the individual will gain much respect and manageability of the unit. The many qualities previously outline to define and tailor ones ability to managed good interpersonal skills are important and should be implemented throughout ones career. In addition to the qualities mention, it really comes down to the effectiveness of how the individual can wisely choose the words to get a predetermined result.

## My Reflection On Words!

*I wanted to take back what I said to him but I didn't. My palms began to sweat and my heart raced for me to say something. I did not. I could see his eyes swell with pain of my words. Suddenly, the spirit in me sent a burst of energy to do what moments before I could not: Please forgive me,—I wish not to use words to hurt you so, only to express my point of view, I finally said. We acknowledge the wrong and begin to heal—with no painful words to imprison us of not getting to the true purpose.—N. Anderson.*

In the poem, *Words! Words!* by Jessie Redmon Fauset, it made me reflect the many experiences I personally express to those whom I love, through words.

Jessie Redmon Fauset is a unique poetic writer born on April 27, 1882 in Frederickville, New Jersey, to a Minister of the African Methodist Episcopal Church in Snow Hill, an all black community founded by Quakers as a home for escaped slaves. When she was still a young child the family moved to Philadelphia, Jessie went to the Philadelphia High School for Girls and years later attended Cornell University. Her close ties to W.E.B Du Bois provided her with a teaching job at Fisk University and subsequently became her mentor. In 1918, The Crisis hired her where she worked as a literary editor and the manager editor in W.E.B Du Bois absence. She traveled and did graduate work during this period as well, spending a summer at the Sorbonne and receiving her M.A. from the University of Pennsylvania in 1919. She also moved to Harlem in 1919 and her outstanding accomplishments through fiction and non-fiction literature: Jessie Redmon Fauset became one of the Black Elite Women of the Harlem Renaissance.

She also helped launch many of the other well known poets and writers from this time period from Langston Hughes to Jean Toomer, in which, she became their mentors. Jessie is known and documented of her poetry to reflect a sense of rhyme and meter. In my own analysis of her poems, I discovered she not only used the method of rhyming and meter but also a romancing approach to her poetry. In regards, to expressing many different ways we choose to live our lives and the turmoil we feel when those struggles are too much to bear. I feel that is why much of her poems express life from the journey of just living to the rites of passage of death.

The method of Jessie's poems emulates the ever interchanging of emotions relating to life. My selection of this particular poem from Jessie to highlight the significance of words and how we choose to use them, did in fact, evoke an emotion in me to share with others—which the sole purpose of poets and writers. The poem expresses the need to remember just why we as souls unite and rediscover the love we have between us rather than expressing words in an un-joyful expression. This poem is the one that you can come back too time and time again in order of regrouping for the sheer purpose of remembering—to just love.

In this chapter, I will give focus on the following areas of specifics that make up the umbrella of developing and sustaining good interpersonal skills.

## A. Practicing the Golden Theme.

*The Primary Team:*

1. The manager and the co-worker.
2. You and your manager.
3. You and your immediate co-worker.

## B. Issues preventing to reach Diversity

*All parties that make up Corporate America:*

1. Corporate America initiative towards diversity.
2. Management responsibilities to employees.
3. Employees respecting other employees on the same level.

## C. Understanding Personal Issues from Professional Agendas.

*Staying away from Sexual Harassment to Verbal Abuse:*

1.Corporate America commitment for safety to their employees.
2.Management responsibility.
3.Employees' duty to all parties in contact with in day-to-day activities at work.

## A. Practicing the Golden Theme

Treat those the way you wish to be treated. Choose wisely on when to fight your battles.

*The Primary Team:*

### 1.The manager and the co-worker.

Power can change our ability to understand the real issue at hand. Management is at a level of not only directing the unit it manages but also the leader representing respect, professionalism, and the integral part of Corporate America. Listen to your employees and communicate effectively when it is good news or bad news to your employees. Place yourself in the employee's position and remember how you respond positively when you are respected and honored.

Remember, if you want your team to be a team you must lead with fairness and understanding of the unit fundamentals goals and future initiative to direct your team effectively—this is mastering respect and congratulating all team members for coming into work every day and making an effort to reach set goals. Numbers are important to make and those that exceed is wonderful but also the team at a whole that puts in an effort. This understanding should be implement into your daily managing of the unit to develop a strong solid team.

We will review a couple of experiences that happens in Corporate America and analyze the situation:

**Episode 1:**

Ted and Janet were called into the conference room with their manager Rose concerning the Williams' account. Ted and Janet have kept wonderful notes and are ready for the meeting. Rose finally enters the conference room and takes her seat.

*"Ted, I just got off the phone with Deidre Johnson the Head Office Manager, and she is very upset with the results so far. What is going on?"*

*"Janet and I have continued to strive to bring down the outstanding dollars of this account, but the hold up is in the database not allowing us to access sufficient records in order to recoup all moneys due. However, the system seems to be corrected and we have shown some progress."*

*"I need all of the major results now, no excuses."*

*"But Ted and I have produced sufficient numbers weekly. We both have come up with a spreadsheet to track..."*

*"I don't believe I was talking to you yet, Janet. Ted you were chosen to lead this project, and I expected in this opportunity. It has been two weeks, and I need this project completed."*

~ ~ ~

Ok, what part do you think needs to improve on interpersonal skills? There are a couple golden opportunities that Rose has missed the big picture in motivating her team. Rose failed in several areas of listening to her employees. Instead, she is high on the power trip and frustrated because she couldn't calm the Head Office Manager. The main problem preventing for lack of high results was the database issues, and Rose should have spent more time looking into getting it resolved. Did she ask for the worksheets that Ted and Janet had to show their progress? Even though it the desired goal wasn't met, nonetheless, they were making progress. Did she stop to realize that her stressed and uncaring attitude towards her employees by talking to Janet that way would only leave the infrastructure of the team in disarray?

These frictions will most undoubtedly leave employees to want to post out or leave the company completely. No employee appreciates a tight schedule with un-relentless pressure. And to top it off the manager is giving out demands right and left not honoring your feelings as a human being and your dedicated effort to try and make a difference. The manager must listen to their employees and use encouraging words that will soothe the stress of the team and motivate them to continue striving towards a successful reached goal.

~~~

**Episode 2:**

When power clouds the vision of respecting your team members, the manager speaks and acts negatively to certain team members that will cause bad impressions. Another Episode below will bring this more into focus:

*"Shari let Bobby teach you the daily procedures to you and not Charlotte because she is still struggling with the job duties."*

Charlotte's back is turned but she is still in hearing distance of what her manager just said. She bit her lip trying to hold her rising emotional state of self worth, her place in the team, and what her manager values of the team.

~ ~ ~

The problem here is the lack of consideration from the manager. This is a big no-no to publicly speak on one of your employee's performance levels in front of other team members. The state of mind the manager has now placed on Charlotte is wrong because she should never feel her self worth is beneath the rest of the team. If Charlotte is not getting the job duties by a sufficient amount of time, then the manager should have had a counseling time with Charlotte to discuss other options, even transfer to another department. The key to remember here is don't abuse your power by disrespecting your team members and then wonder why they are not following you, speaking to you, or better yet if they choose to leave the company.

### 2. You and your manager.

Honor the position that your manager has in the unit but never over step your boundaries. You are an important part of the unit and must also be honored and respected. Go to your manager with issues that exceed your capabilities instead of going outside of your unit. Perhaps you already know that another manager might have the answer but use caution.

Most managers don't take kind to their employees going outside their unit or above their heads. Finally, always listen clearly to what is being said by your manager and develop clearly your responses to the advancement of the team.

Lets review a couple of episodes for the above area of focus:

**Episode 1:**

The manager has had several team meetings covering the normal updates going on affecting the team. In addition, the manager has mentioned each time in these meetings concerning the issue about staying out of their desk and department areas for long lengths of time. Two employees are the main ones who are doing this act but still are violating what the manager has implemented. One day, the manager called one by one of the two to a conference to discuss this issue.

*"I was only getting me some water and was stopped by another employee."* *Walter said.*

*"But it was 45 minutes that you were away from your desk, in which, calls were not being answered but routing to someone else." The manager said.*

The main problem here is honesty from the employee. The employee knows that he is at fault and has not taken responsibilities to adhere to the department policy. Walter should have admitted his wrong and apologize for not doing as the manager requested. He should have indicated to the manager that this type of behavior will not continue and guarantee that improvement will be noticed. The company is paying you for timed worked not timed socialized with your friends.

~ ~ ~

**Episode 2:**

*"Beth, I noticed that you received a lot of personal calls and that you stayed on the phone for long periods of time."*

*"I don't believe they were really considered personal calls, most of them were problems with my utility company and bank that I couldn't resolve but during normal office hours."*

This might be true for the employee but it should have been handled more professionally. Indicate to your manager of this crisis at home and that personal calls will have to be made. Explanation will garner you not only permission but also understanding your needed time for flexibility.

### 3. You and your immediate co-worker.

The primary team is you and the people who are working under the same immediate supervisor to accomplish a certain goal for the unit. This unit is very important because you will interact with the team on a daily basis. Your primary objective is first keeping your balance of emotions. Do not let anyone alter your state. I know there are times when occurrences happen that makes your face turn red or green, but you must be the bigger person. Also, keep in mind that whoever is the agitator that you are going to clean your slate.

How do you clean your slate? Take responsibility and be honest. Most of the drama between you and your co-worker is excess baggage that individuals are dropping on you. Give back the baggage and move on.

If you still need to cool off, take a moment or day or two to do just that, but you must and I do stress this that you have to be professional.

This means that you must interact with the individual and rise above the incident. Many of times I have found myself in an incident that I felt the individual was unfair in the ordeal. Once I calmed down, I went to the individual and asked for assistance on a case I needed help on. I wiped off the dirt and healed my scar to focused on the job at hand. Simply put, I moved on.

Keep communication going. If the incident prolongs or increases to an explosive experience have a meeting with you two and the immediate manager for a resolution.

**Things to remember in developing positive relations:**

1. Mind your own business. Have your focus on the job at hand and don't gossip.

2. Listen to the other person's statements clearly and respond professionally.

3. Always say thank you when getting assistance.

4. Show concern to your co-worker when a crisis is affecting their attitude.

5. Take credit, when it is done by you but be respectful.

6. Give credit to those who really achieved results for the unit.

7. Don't tell the supervisor of your issue. First go to that person and try handling it.

~ ~ ~

Now, lets proceed to the next area focus in this series of developing and sustaining good interpersonal skills.

## B. Issues preventing to reach Diversity

*All parties that make up Corporate America:*

### 1.Corporate America initiative towards diversity.

To be a unified source of business presence you must understand fully what diversity adds to your company. Adapting a sound philosophy that is trustworthy and honoring employees that are from different cultures, race and/or religious beliefs will sustain your company's foundation a hundred folds. One of the best diversity company statement and mission was from the official website of Chase Manhattan Bank. It demonstrated a professional and sincere approach towards diversity in the work place. The company should always have a specific company view on diversity in the mission statement. The company should have meetings or set up a specialized committee to oversee issues concerning minorities at your company. This committee's main focus should be to implementation in developing professional skills as well as bringing culture differences to other employees and the company initiative.

~ ~ ~

## Episode 1: A catch 20-20

*"Marshal, I strongly feel that I am in a corner for my team leader has it in for me, and our manager sides with whatever the leader says."*

*"Cynthia just try to go to the Humans Resources department about our team leader."*

*"But then HR could notify our manager and tell that it was me who was bringing this problem up. Forget that, I know HR will not listen especially since I am a minority and then I will be brand named as a problem employee and will get bad treatment. I just feel so trapped."*

~ ~ ~

Most major companies have a specific 800 number for all employees to call into and report any unethical practices by management or unsalaried employees. This is an excellent resource for individuals who strongly feel their immediate supervisor is in a conflicting position to talk to. Cynthia should try and see an 800-compliance number is available in HR before she is pushed to leave the department or the company because of the continuing stressful atmosphere. Taking the time to review all available sources that Corporate has before assuming there is no option can be a missed opportunity to resolve the issues. In addition, Cynthia could see if another manager would be helpful to listen to the situation that she feels she can trust—in order to talk out Cynthia's options and confirm her suspicions that HR personal would not help the situation.

### Episode 2: Racism

There is sometimes a fear of approaching HR when the issue relies on race. This is a touchy subject and sometimes hard to prove to the parties that are involved. The key to overcome this is keeping documentation. Good documentation with dates, incidents, and the situation that caused the problem to occur. Believe it or not there are many different ways to exercise racism and bigotry in the workplace these days. The key for

Corporate is to realize the trends and the methods being done to enforce this negative expression to employees.

*"Terrell, is it just me? In the whole division I only see one black team leader and no black manager or any African-American in a high position." Bob said before taking a bite out of his sandwich."*

*"I see the same thing and not just in our division but the whole building only has a few minorities in lead positions, and I do mean a few. I think there is one Latino manager in the mail room."*

~ ~ ~

This is can be interpreted in many different ways, but trust me these types of conversations go on all the time in the workplace and the belief is there to monitor and draw a conclusion. How do the company assure to minority employees that racism doesn't exist? By having a diversity network set up to make sure awareness of what employees are feeling and any reports of discriminations are being performed in departments. These resources will provide employees and Corporate to make sure fairness of the evaluations of skills, knowledge and dedication for desired advancement are being measured by all individuals in the company.

Corporate can have unique seminars set up regularly during the year to encourage employees to speak up on unethical practices of racism. Many other seminars are conducted to focus on team building skills but rarely you find seminars particularly focusing on this issue. Even though the company has an EOE policy, the company must implement seminars to showcase employees what not to do in a situation that could be considered racist. Teaching the effectiveness of how to relate to individuals who are of different culture is crucial in helping your employees develop strong interpersonal skills. The employees will be able to relate to the contents in the seminar that the type of behavior will not be tolerated and Corporate is listening to better their company.

As Corporate focuses on this topic and implements sessions for continued non-tolerance, so shall the managers that directs and leads employees in their division. The managers will also learn the many tangles of web to not lead astray or violate employee potential rights. In addition, literature needs to be available that lists important numbers to contact such violated rules and helpful measures of situations to avoid and watch out for.

Below is a poem that focuses on diversity and geared towards reflection within the world:

### An Opal of Color

I stared deeply into my eyes as tears formed

I couldn't wait till the day will end—and I could be born, again.

I touched my woolly hair and then my face and nose

And wish I could become like those I see praise,

I felt my color would not allow me to be raised to that level of beauty

I bit my lower lip to hide my need to scream,

I saw in the mirror the pain in my eyes; I quickly closed them.

I wished the night would come for me to hide,
When a voice from behind spoke with love:

"You are the Opal of Color, be not as others, but as what you were born to be,

You are blessed my child, love your image."

My god, my god, I screamed as the tears streamed down my face

Forgive me, for forgetting my heritage, at which was a gift to me

I looked into my eyes,

They bloomed as a sparkling dark color gem

And my skin glowed as an opal with rims of color

I smiled, the love entering my once broken heart

I began to be a proud new me—a woman of color.

Nichel Anderson

~ ~ ~

## 2. Management responsibilities to employees

Fully understanding the corporate diversity mission statement is very important in being effective to your diversified employees. You can approach each situation with ease of understanding the sometimes-touchy situations when you must address an issue. Respecting others' differences and culture will make you a better player. Listening to your employees and placing yourself in their position will encourage you to make your decisions wisely without contradicting corporate diversity initiative.

**Episode 1:**

*"Jennifer, you are doing such an excellent job on the files for the downtown office."*

*"Thank you, but Julie helped me as well." Tom said.*

*The manager gave a quick un-interested grin and then went back to his office.*

*"Thanks Jennifer for speaking up for me but don't bother. He always ignores what I contributed to any thing I do for the department. It is really getting on my nerves."*
*"I am beginning to think it is more than an oversight, Julie."*

*"Yeah, the oversight is blatant ignoring my contributions but hey, I am the only Mexican American here. So I don't have a loud voice to complain and make a difference for a change."*

~ ~ ~

This is a classic scenario even when there is only one minority in the immediate office. People notice the way management treats certain people compared to others. Make sure you are complimenting all employees who have contributed to a project not a particular person all the time. Especially when the one who never seems to get much or any credit is a minority, the end result will be felt and understood that racism exists in the company. Another focus to keep in mind is to not be phony when you are congratulating employees leaving an impression that you have to do it rather than you genuinely want to give praise.

Trust me this type of method can be easily interpreted and not appreciated. The employee will still feel that racist views still exist in the work place. You should understanding the right way to motivate and direct your team in a fair and influential way, the one who leads effectively will have a strong following. Remembering the golden rule will apply great here; to treat those the way you wish to be treated.

Let us look at another scenario to develop and sustain better interpersonal relations.

### 3. Employees respecting other employees on the same level

Having respect for your immediate co-workers' differences will enable you to develop stronger relationships to your team members. You should always honoring others feelings during conversations of either about the work or during a luncheon when you must chat to relax and relieve stress is crucial in developing good interpersonal skills. The wonderful benefit of learning to work well with employees will precede you into a better world rounded individual as well as an employee.

### Episode 1:

*"Didn't you hear what was rolled out in the last meeting on how to do R130 report? What is wrong with you are you dumb or something?" Janet rolled her eyes as she walked back to her desk.*

*"I'm sorry Janet that I messed up the point but to be honest, I really didn't understand the steps to generate that report." Harry said.*

*Janet looked up at the ceiling in annoyance. "You never get anything right."*

The issue here happens a lot in Corporate America where one employee needs reassuring of self and to reach this level of assurance they take punch shots at another employee. Not to say that there are times when an employee continues to not grasp the job duties, but there are ways to effectively get your message across for improvement and sustaining good interpersonal relationships with co-workers.

Instead of being negative, approach the situation with calmness in order to gain control of the issue:

*"Harry, if you want, sometime this week I can go over the steps with you and perhaps breakdown the lingo in layman's terms. And if we go over it several times I know that you will get it because repetition is always the best way of learning something new and foreign." Janet said with a pleasant smile.*

*"Thanks Janet, that would be so nice of you. Honestly, I really felt pressure to getting the new procedures for running the report when it is much better for to learn new things if they were written down and with examples." replied Harry.*

Most people don't master this level of keeping good relations with the co-workers whom you closely work with, instead, burned bridges occur and uncomfortable situations happen because of animosity.

~ ~ ~

**Episode 2:**

*"Why don't you just ask Timothy to show you to interpret the spreadsheet?"*

*"You know why. He is a jerk and always showing off in our team meetings. I won't give him the satisfaction."*

*"So what are you going to do, Rita?"*

*"Bob is due back from vacation on Wednesday. I will wait until then."*

*"But I thought, Bob said he might not return on Wednesday and that he might come back a week later."*

*Rita shrugged her shoulders.*

This is a classic case where bridges have been burned and the comfort zone is no more between closely worked co-workers. In Corporate America, this type of behavior cannot exist for long due to the need of the team to be solid. Therefore, one of these two employees who are at odds must be the bigger person. I personally would decide to look past my differences with a person whom we did not get along with personally and think of the prime objective; the business initiative.

Instead of fuming or wasting time and money not completing your job task, get up and force a smile to get the answers you need in order to get the job done. Think of business. Not personal issues. Sometimes this is very hard to do mainly because of continued bad experiences you might have with the other person. But you must gain the strength and heart to move past the bad feelings—even for awhile—and communicate professionally with the co-worker by staying on focus to the initiative relating to your job.

Over time the other person will secretly respect you because the other person knows that there are still bad feelings brewing but admire your ability to being untouched by the previous negative experience. Moreover, you will feel great for standing up to the challenge and succeeding in Corporate America that entails multiple personalities to get along with or better yet mastering the ability to seeing the bigger picture. Capturing this essence will benefit you in the long run when you are promoted or lead a particular project. Your focus will be where it should be, and upper management will notice your quality to stay calm when turmoil surrounds you. This type of quality is a must for any lead position because with calmness a person has direction and determination. Having direction and determination in Corporate America is like having a plate of gold because you rise above all occasions of different situations. And that is a vital characteristic.

~ ~ ~

## C. Understanding The Differences Of Personal Issues from Professional Agendas.

*Staying away from Sexual Harassment to Verbal Abuse:*

### 1. Corporate America commitment to safety for their employees

Listening to your employees when a manager has violated the company's stated policy of no tolerances of bad behavior is crucial in developing loyal employees. Yes, the normal protocol is for the channel of command to be adhered to—but most of the time the manager the employee must report to first is bias to the situation due to favoritism of the manager in question. Implementing an open door policy will be beneficial to you and to your employees in preventing issues as disturbing as sexual harassment and verbal abuse. Conduct more regular seminars of no tolerance for such bad behavior, in order, to encourage those to speak up and seek help. Honor each employee, as they so deserve with respect and care because the employee needs to feel they matter.

Lets look at an episode to further review:

**Episode 1:**

*"I'm not sure if I should go to the VP of human resources, I was told that the HR department here doesn't listen to employees. They only back up management. And after the response I got from this office site human resources manager, I feel I am in a catch 20-20,"* Carol said as she stirred her coffee while sitting in the company break room.

*"I heard the same thing. Perhaps you should get a lawyer to get some justice for unwanted sexual advances. You should not feel victimize. And if you have no other alternative,"* Frieda replied.

*"You know, I think that is a good idea. I am going to get a lawyer and talk over my options,"* Carol responded before taking a sip of her coffee.

~ ~ ~

Most employees rather go outside of the company base to assist in a crisis, and I can understand their position because I felt trapped in a situation that seemed to have no way out. In these times, I often consulted with individuals I know I can trust. My confidants are also ones who are professional and can see all angles that are involved to help lead me on the right path. I still make the final decision but talking out the situation and listening to other alternatives to take will help you in choosing wisely.

**Options You Should Take**

Consider communicating with the individual in question, in order, for you to make clear your stand and purpose for working at the company. One approach is writing to reach your objective that the for-said behavior and advances will not be tolerated. Talking is another way of making the lines between the two of you clear but at times could be tricky.

This is because later on if the occurance continues, you have no solid proof of what was said or anything that was done in accordance. It is safe to say written will be the number one option to clear any encouragement of misbehavior in the workplace on your part. The letter can be short and to the point with a positive tone. Remember, if the situation continues and escalates this is your proof—that you tried to settle the matter on your level before asking for higher management to intercede.

Try the below approach by sending an email. All companies' emails become the property of corporate and can be easily re-tracked at any given time. This is okay because you want to be able to have documentation to back up your claim of misconduct.

Try the below approach:

*Good Morning Steve,*

*The last time we encountered one another in the elevator has lead me to insist that any further communication should be strictly business related. Your unwarranted phone messages, notes on my computer, and emails requesting to have lunch or dinner must stop immediately. I strongly feel this is inappropriate behavior in a business setting where we both work and in which, I have indicated to you that I am uninterested anything other than business related matters. If further action in this regard continues I will have to seek assistance from higher management.*

*Sincerely,*
*Carol Wobleson*
*Lolleson Mutual*

If the situation does continue, your immediate supervision should be consulted. When it seems that your immediate manager and next upper manager will not listen, you should try to consult with a representative in human resources. Don't get upset if they send you back to your manager, this is common so don't panic. Call a meeting with your immediate manager first. In this initial meeting write down the concerns being conflicting to focus on the job task. In the episode just presented, tailored what you want to say to what you need to say. Indicate your need to clarify the expectations from an employee and employer. If the meeting does not give a good feeling that things will change, you will need to call another meeting with your supervisor and upper management to proceed with your concerns. Provide documentation of all scenarios that proves your position of extreme concern and tailor your words that are not confrontational but on a level that present only of your sincerity to getting back to business.

~ ~ ~

## 2. Management responsibility

Be aware of the words you use to your employees and always think on the level of professionalism. Sometimes this is hard when we joke during the day and become comfortable with our colleagues. The comfortable zone can be an awarding experience when days seem so stressful but the zone can also be a dangerous one. Remember to keep your mind focused even when you are relaxing with your employees. What you might feel is okay might not be kosher to the employee, and you will then be in a catch 20-20 in explaining your actions or comments to an upper management. Take note on the way you congratulate your employee. Never continue to call the employee for a medial task that is obvious just to be around that employee. Watch out for the way you use any type of physical appreciation. This can be misleading and misinterpreted. What was done in your household when you grew up may not be the same way the employee was taught to show appreciation of a job well done. You must understand that in Corporate America the rules are in place that such behavior either intentionally or not will not be tolerated.

Lets review another episode for further review:

**Episode 1:**

*"Well I think you are the problem Selia not the rest of the team and how is the gossip getting spread amongst the team?"*

*"Betty I would not have brought this issue up if I didn't feel this type of behavior is preventing me to feeling comfortable and getting my job done. I should not have to be treated badly by being belittled or insensitive remarks being made about my work due to that rumor. I am coming to you for a resolution of the problem and that is why I am here in your office to do something about this matter."*

As managers, the golden rule of treating those like you would want to be treated can be forgotten. The golden rule is vital in managing employees in Corporate America to have a team that will back you when you need them too. Keep an open mind and focus on the problem being presented by your employee. Show interests in what the employee is expressing is an extreme concern and suggest a one and one conference meeting between both employees and offer for you to sit in as third party. Encourage this meeting in the mission to resolve the issues being presented in the team. Expressing good listening skills will instill in the people whom you manage—that you possess great leadership and the devotion to professionalism as well as being fair to all parties on the team.

If you hear all sides and equally try to make your decision on the facts and the right direction to lead the team, the prime objective of the unit will be reach successfully by getting the team back on course. Stay away from favoritism that often clouds most managers' judgment and rather look at the team as a whole. Place each individual accountable of the area that they are strong at for that is the definition of any successful team. When you take sides all the time, it instills to other members of the team that they can't come to you with any issues. In response, the individual will take the issues outside of your unit. And I'm sure that is not what you rather happen, the route preferred is for the manager to take care of their internal issues of the unit successfully.

～ ～ ～

## 3. Employee's duty to all parties in contact in day-to-day activities at work.

Believing that closeness and the persuasion to flirt here and there will get you somewhere…you should think again. This is a dangerous route. Corporate can be a force to be reckon with when their policy has been violated. *Why?* Because other employees who are always watching and spreading office rumors will have so many lawsuits of favoritism and discrimination against the company your head will spin. This practice of persuasion to get you up the corporate ladder does not work in the long haul. The risks are too high to take a chance because it is much better to focus on your job duties and exceeding the right way instead of partaking in a dangerous dance.

～ ～ ～

## Keeping Yourself Motivated In Corporate America

What keeps me motivated and focused on my journey is that I forgive those who are ignorant of selfish tactics that affect my emotional state. Instead, I choose to rise above and roll off the negative and get back to enjoying the journey. Poetry plays a great deal in strengthen me, one poem in particular is by Maya Angelou, *I still rise*. Recently, I wrote an essay thanking Maya for writing such a beautiful poem and provided my own reflection of what her essay meant to me. Maya's essay encouraged me to see above the many challenges I encounter day to day. Although, I know what I must do by moving forward—reading such beautiful poetry that truly relates to my feelings keeps my heart filled with positive energy and gives me the strength to keep moving forward on my journey.

My essay on staying on course when facing adversity:

## And Still I Rise

*I remember a beautiful day like this…*

The movements of the clouds made me want to reach up to the sky and touch them. The birds continued singing a mystical melody that filled my soul with hope and promise. That day was a beautiful day, for it was a new beginning as the soft grass underneath me cushions my body with love and devotion. Tree branches were moving right and left to feather a cool breeze to my brow. Yes, it was a new beginning in order to set a new path for my dreams.

*My dreams are many.* They are combined with my ancestors' memories of hopes and sealed with their legacy. Yes, I have dreams to be the very best in whatever that I choose to accomplish in life. Looking above into the heavens that wonderful spring day encouraged me to dream bigger dreams and not let anyone prevent my vision for evolving into being.

Blue skies anew and old taught me how beautiful growing can be and how fulfilling to one's soul. I engulfed having the courage to obtain such beauty being surrounded by gracefulness. Yes, I have dreams to not worry about the naysayer but direct my own path. To not listen to those destined to test my wisdom, courage, and love of self on my journey of living but to rise to the occasion of a challenge.

A cloud full of plumpness and depth winked at me. *I listen to the wind.* The wind flew up and around me with urgency. The sheer lining of the wind movements perked up the hairs on my arm. *I continued to listen and wait.* The wind hollered at me to take caution and listen to some of those voices, for they might be harsh but wise to lead me to safer ground.

I eyed the wind that surrounded me with no face, and no body but a determined voice.

I know of those voices that speak harshly and claim of good will. *I listen to my spirit to guide me in the right direction.* At times, those voices can utter truth and wisdom, and at other times those voices can turn bitter and mean, in order to stop me from moving forward. The voices say one thing, but their intentions are really to twist and misinterpret my legacy, my heritage, and my freedom of expression.

The voices became filled with jealousy and vile contempt that thrushes against my spirit to bring me down. The voices push and taint me in order to destroy what I have built. Those voices can be disguised with warmth but really convey a mission to lead me astray.

The wind curled up underneath my nose to tickle the courage that continued to build inside me. *I laid still.*

Many journeys by others are accomplished successfully making this path, and I choose to move forward. I choose to stand my ground. I choose to have love of self and express this love to others. With my mighty spirit from the creator of the heavens, I am strong enough to move forward. I will evolve to what my ancestors dreamed for me to become; a loving spirit of creativity.

The wind came up and brushed against my body and whirled a tunnel of force around me. The forceful currents of the wind seemed to hurled words of breezes to taunt my wisdom and strength. The trees waved in the clouds to come and protect me. However, the wind came down with such thunder on a fierce mission to blow me away. The grass strands near my feet and arms could measure the depth of the fall of the wind. The grass danced a jubilee rhythm to protect my body from the approaching thunder.

Looking into the faceless wind…*and still I rise* with courage to move forward in my journey of living.

~ ~ ~

Maya has a burst of laughter that portrays to me strength and wisdom towards living. Not to mention she is my mentor because her high spirit encourages a person to laugh away the troubles of life and continue to enjoy the journey. I love all of her literary work but the most favorite one of all by Maya that I adore, is *Still I Rise* poem. It exemplifies what I feel life challenges are and what I feel to being empowered to succeed. Many days are like what I described in my essay concerning life's obstacles and Maya's poem helps me to understand the true meaning of such things…to get back up and knock those forces down that are trying to prevent you in achieving success.

Poetry is giving of one spirit and bountiful soul in order to enrich others. Love is woven through poetry because it comes from the heart of the poet to move another one's spirit. Maya's poem delivers the poignant force to raise you above the challenges in order to reach your dreams.

Having inspiring quotes or poetry around your desk to reinforce your mission to sustain a good attitude is a wonderful way of enjoying your journey. Think of the many things that make you smile and regain your composure and implement these measures in your every day attempt to make it a brighter day. Listen to your needs and answer them by finding ways that supports your efforts to being a better person as well as having a better working environment in Corporate America.

Show honor to yourself by rolling off negative energy and being an example for those who are having great difficulty on the journey. Always have the understanding that you are not alone on this quest to rising above, and being empowered to making a difference in other's lives as well as in your own…is the key towards success.

Success is measured by how you overcome the situations that challenges you to fall backward, in which, you choose to push forward on your journey. In return, the doors will open and you will reach the level of achievement that you so desired. And that is a great thing. At times it can be really difficult moving ahead because you are so boggled down with stress, if this is the case, you should think about taking a trip in order to sustain good interpersonal skills and gain back your self-empowerment status quo.

## Soft Breezes To Soothe Your Soul

Weary eyes and tired feet could result from stress build up in our lives, and we need to stop and reflect internally the accumulations of issues adding onto our Self.

Many of us ignore the first warning signs and even the most glaring signs leading to physical health problems. This is often the case when the spirit has tried the simple way of letting us know to slow down and now it is on the verge of shutting down; therefore, more vivid signs are present. There are many booklets on the market to help prepare us mentally and spiritually to live better lives. And the most often used answer to that option is time, and a person is just too busy or too scared to admit that something is wrong with them.

But in this stage of the game relating to spiritual health, time is an important factor and of the essences, but also your choice to live in a peaceful state should be the number one priority.

Take the time that you need to refocus your priorities. Take the time to really enjoy living. It starts with having a solid foundation of being connected to your soul that is being housed by your spirit. Love will flourish once you take 30 minutes alone and just listen…to the silence—preferably sitting in front of an open window to absorb the sun and breeze. Spirit will speak. Your soul will jump forth and introduce itself or re-introduce itself, and a whole new world will open up to you. And in this new awakening, you should allow the soft breezes to soothe your soul. All the freedom to reconnect to your inner self will be before you so you can start living.

Many of us need more time to reconnect, and there are great places around the world to do just that. They are designed to cater to your inner self, with no worries of the guilt of being selfish, but rather allowing you to love yourself—a place where your spirit can beam with brightness. It is that time again when the weather is changing to a warm sunny breeze. The blooms of once fall plants are beginning to paint the neighborhood with color. Now the decision is not only what bathing suit to buy but where you take your loved one to reconnect with your spirit on a much-needed vacation.

A great place to do this is no other than the #1 couple spot in the world: Sandals Royal Bahamian Resort & Spa, located in the Bahamas on Nassau's world-renowned Cable Beach.

The Sandals Royal Bahamian Resort & Spa is the most elegant and impressive of all-inclusive resorts, combining the majestic architectural style of Europe with the sensual passion of island breezes.

The resort has been magnificently decorated with Romanesque statues and Grecian urns. The gardens are lavishly arranged throughout the resort to ease even the most restless individual. The entryway and lobby are ornately decorated with marble columns and floors, with extraordinary artwork on the ceilings and the hanging paintings. The feeling that will surely engulf you when entering this resort is pure comfort.

The Sandals Royal Bahamian Resort & Spa has the most luxurious living quarters in the Caribbean, from beachfront rooms and villas to suites. Each area is uniquely decorated with handcrafted mahogany furnishings. And all suites come with the unparalleled exclusive services of your own Suite Concierge who will cater to your every whim, morning, noon, and night. The special Suite Concierge Program provides privileges such as V.I.P check-in and extra touches such as his and her terry cloth robes.

With any vacation in the Caribbean, the scenery is a must-have and Sandals Royal Bahamian Resort & Spa is very satisfying. The resort has a gorgeous main pool; it is the islands only heated pool. The second pool is located on Sandals' offshore island, Balmoral, where you can escape and enjoy the endless stretch of white-sand beach and the Caribbean sun. In addition, the resort has three additional private mini-pools for intimate moments together. If you and your loved one need your aches and pains to be readjusted then try the swirling sensation of one of the four whirlpools surrounded by classical statues. Or you can energize your spirits and refresh your body in the islands' only genuine misting pool. This mist water will surely soothe all of your worries under the beautiful sun.

Also, try some exercise to get your heart pumping with a fierce spirit towards living. The resort provides snorkeling, water skiing and even scuba diving, not to mention sailing, canoeing, paddle boating, kayaking, windsurfing and glass-bottom boat rides to tickle your fancy. It's all included along with the state-of-the-art equipment and professional instruction.

The Sandals Royal Bahamian Resort & Spa is the ultimate vacation spot for an adventurous and soothing experiences this summer. Make it a grand affair for yourself, and I guarantee that you will feel rejuvenated with a powerful spirit to live life with confidence, courage and joy!

~ ~ ~

I went to my most closest co-workers I encountered in working in Corporate America and asked them what favorite quote or passage of a poem motivated them. These were of the best of many that I accumulated from my query and perhaps will enrich your spirit—to begin each day in Corporate America with a wonderful attitude towards yourself and others that will enhance your self-empowerment and sustain good interpersonal skills.

## Favorite Quotes Most Corporate Workers Live By To Ease Away Stress:

"Smart people learn from their mistakes, brilliant people learn from other's mistakes."—Aaron Harris, Graduate of University of Florida.

~ ~ ~

"Whatever you do, work at it with all your heart, as working for the Lord, not for men, since you know that you will receive an inheritance from the Lord as a reward. It is the Lord Christ you are serving. Anyone who does wrong will be repaid for his wrong and there is no favoritism." Colossians 3:23-25—Kimberly Young, Analyst

~ ~ ~

"If there are no bad times in our life—We would not appreciate the good times."—Donna Waide, Bad Dept Finanical Analyst

~ ~ ~

"Never again will I confess fear, for God hath not given me the spirit of fear, but of power and of love, and of a sound mind."—Timothy 1:7—Sandra Wilson, Unpaid Claims Report Analyst.

**Cont. Favorite Quotes Most Corporate Workers Live By To Ease Away Stress:**

~ ~ ~

"Manners will take you places money won't."—Angelia Smith, Research and Correspondance Department

~ ~ ~

I press toward the mark for the prize of the high calling of God in Christ Jesus.—Philippians 3:14 King James Version.—Vinita Stokes, Discrepancy Analyst

~ ~ ~

Open your eyes, and look within. Are you satisfied with the life you're living?—a phrase from the song Exodus by Bob Marley—Angela Robinson, Financial Analyst

~ ~ ~

Emancipate yourselves from mental slavery, only but ourselves can free our minds.—a song lyric by Bob Marley.—Andrea Means, Special Project Coordinator

~ ~ ~

Keeping your heart clear of negative energy will allow you to enjoy your experience while in Corporate America—in which, your journey will be an enjoyable one. Understanding other's feelings and what makes them tick to be motivated, the workplace will become productive and with great respect to those who are apart of the team. Developing and mastering great interpersonal skills is the key to a successful coexistence in Corporate America…leading to wonderful opportunities of enriching relationships both professionally and personally.

# PART THREE

# Obtaining Your Professional Empowerment

# CHAPTER 5

# Making A Statement With Your Appearance

Everyone wants to achieve the highest recognition, the impression to set a style to be remembered by those who hold your career in their hands. In order to achieve this level of achievement you must understand the fundamentals of organizing, buying smart, and planning your wardrobe in Corporate America. On this level of mastery, the skies are the limit. And trust me, your clothes define who you are and that is very important in the competitive business arena. Making a statement with your appearance may seem like an easy task for most, however, an effective appearance is a balance of knowing what is appropriate in the workplace and being within the workplace guidelines.

Take for instance; a company might have a policy for business casual everyday. This type of policy can be tricky to interpret what is allowed and what is not allowed. In addition, the company might have a policy that is strict and is the professional look. Or perhaps, on certain days, the company will allow Fridays for jeans day. The final dilemma that falls in every decision to being in compliance with the company's policy; the decision to make sure the attire is not too sexy, revealing or controversy.

In this chapter we will explore the policies mentioned by presenting a breakdown of the do's and don'ts in Corporate America. We will also investigate the benefits of dressing for success that will deliver the right and predetermined message to others in the workplace.

## The Professional

Feeling great and able to perform at high performance is known when a person dresses professional, a person who can project a well tailored and mature appearance will command attention and respect. When a person has that respect and attention, the world is at an easier reach for obtaining success. Learning to coordinate by mastering what is appropriate in Corporate America will provide the individual a sense of direction for the future. Being able to stay on the level of professionalism, the individual will always be the leader in the crowd of many.

Lets start by examining the basics and then move on to the exceptional appearance:

- A starched shirt and solid colored skirt is always the #1 approach towards being professional. The other accessories will be stockings and mid-high heels and pearl earrings and a necklace.

- Tailored shirt with a matching tie and tailored pants, the individual will have nice dress shoes with coordinated color socks.

- To finish the look off, add a fine tailored blazer with a color that is appealing and a nice touch.

Now for women wearing slacks and a nice top is acceptable with nice coordinating shoes. Just make sure the slacks are not too tight but rather a nice silhouette fit and tailored if all possible. This professional look will re-enforce your message of dressing appropriately in Corporate America. In addition, the different companies' attire policy might be somewhat flexible, for example in a law firm you know the dress attire will be professional with the above previous mention attire choices. However, in a more relaxed business environment you might be able to wear the three- piece suit etc.

The best bet is to know which policy the particular company follows. Once you are called in for an interview, you should observe actual employees who work there. Try not to stare but glance around at the attire choices and see how they coordinate their clothes. Make sure you don't fall victim that for instance if the company is not a law firm, than the attire policy will allow a laid back approach towards attire. Instead, you should get clarification with management or Human Resources. These sources will most definitely have the set guidelines to what is allowed and what is not allowed. You will have to remember that just because you see fellow employees being relaxed in their attire than you can too—some employees choose to ignore the dress code and wear what they prefer implying to others that it is okay to not follow the rules.

By taking this approach you are not excelling in Corporate America when competition is everything and your ability to follow the set rules. If you wear the appropriate company's attire, upper management will listen to your ideas as well as respect you for following the guidelines set for employees.

## The Professional

*What is not allowed?*

Anytime you feel so comfortable, in which, your focus on the job objective will lack in concentration and high productivity due to a more laid back approach, it is time to rethink your choice of attire for the work-day. Most employers feel this way, and studies have shown that the way we dress does in fact impact our quality and focus on the company's objective. In most instances, the way we dress can either improve your self-esteem or lower our self-esteem. At first this notion might seem over the top, but not really, we are what we eat as the saying goes—and make a statement about ourselves by what we wear. Keeping that in mind will allow you to understand more deeply how to present and deliver your message in Corporate America more effectively.

There is nothing wrong with wearing comfortable clothing but the primary objective is first to see what the company policy states. Then follow them exactly. Then you should make your choices of attire that is comfortable fitting and at the same time your attire will be in compliance to corporate guidelines.

*Attire that is not allowed in Corporate America:*

- *Tight fitted clothes.* No matter what the company policy states—a person wearing clothes that are too tight is a sure give away of un-professionalism. People will be busy trying to trail your panty lines or the shape of your figure than listen to what you have to say.

- *Clothes too loose.* It might sound odd but it does occur when individuals don't take time in the selection of appropriate sized attire. Choosing this method will present a sloppy presentation. Allow your attire to have a nice silhouette appearance. Anything else will not present a professional image that you wish to make.

- *Non-iron attire.* We can-not allow the lazy bug to persist and have us deliver an inappropriate message. Instead, an individual should iron their upcoming work-week attire days before so the worry of keeping the attire ironed will not be an issue. Also, an individual can start to look for clothes that are wrinkle free even after you wash the attire. Or perhaps the attire after washing only needs a quick warm iron over—then you will still be able to present a professional image. Don't forget that using a reasonable dry cleaning service will also be a great benefit and relieve the task of ironing your clothes.

The primary objective is image, and the clothes that you choose to wear delivers a powerful message: *Success.*

## Business Casual

From a light blue polo shirt and khaki pants to a denim shirt and jeans, the business casual is the most desired dressing attire by employees. The business casual attire is mostly an award by major corporations to provide their workers relaxed feeling from the normal professional image Monday thru Friday routine. The employer promotes the business casual day in order to hopefully improve productivity and employee morale. The employees enjoy this day because it is a wonderful way to feel they are a vital part of the company and it feels great to work in jeans.

Now for the most part, the business casual might be approached easily; however, I have found this can lead to areas that employees should not tread. There are many choices for the employee to make and choosing wisely is crucial in Corporate America.

Lets take a look at some choices and how to make the wise selection. Below are sure winners to invest in:

*Light blue shirt, polo or gap.* This designer shirt tends to be well tailored and the look is what you really want in order to emphasize business casual. Not to say an off brand name will be un-sufficient because an off brand label will work as well. Make you will just have to make sure the look is tailored.

*Khaki pants.* The look is simple but effective. The khaki pants can go with almost any colorful top and still provide you with an impressive business causal look.

*A tee-shirt with heavy fabric.* This is always a good way to be a little more comfortable but not too beyond corporate policy. Along as the fabric is not too thin or transparent, the tee shirt will be a successful accent to your attire.

*Jeans, any name brands.* Wearing jeans is the utmost in comfortability and style; the employee has such a wide selection. I would strongly recommend the basics but always choose the stylish and appropriate colors: blue, dark blue, black or white. Any other color will tend to be too causal and remember we are focused on *business* casual.

## Business Casual

*What is not allowed?*

*Capri pants:* They come in all colors that are pants with lengths a few inches from the knees. For the weekend and the company gathering functions, yes, but during the normal work week these stylist pants need not be worn on a regular business day.

*Shorts:* We all know deep down that this is not good business practice to present a professional appearance. Therefore, this type of attire should never be worn during a business work-week. Not only because it is not appropriate business attire but the question to what is the right length and fit is always a hard way to determine.

*Torn Jeans:* The look is sassy and cool but wear them on the weekend with your friends doing a social gathering together. Do not even consider wearing them on causal Fridays with a minor tear, it is not worth the image you wish to present.

*Tight Jeans:* Always a no, no due to the presentation of not looking professional. When you want to communicate a professional image, the appearance of wearing tight jeans takes the focus off of your intellect and focuses on the jeans you are wearing.

*Low cut shirts:* No matter how flattery this is on you, you should never try and wear a low cut shirt to the workplace. Again your image is to deliver a powerful professional message. You will not deliver that message if excess exposure of skin is extremely showing. Use the old golden rule; if you have to ask and doubt, change your attire.

*Logo Shirts:* In regards to jokes or bad taste logo shirts or tee shirts that might offend a co-worker should also not be worn at work but rather on the weekend on your own time. You do not want to project the wrong perception to those whom you work with daily. Remember how you present yourself, and in this case, your attire, is what you relay to others the way you think. That is crucial in Corporate America.

*Hats:* Saturdays are fine to show your game spirit or at corporate functions; however, the old golden rule also applies. You want to be casual but not too casual and wearing a hat is a no, no inside any building especially at the work.

*Slides:* I love these and have about twenty in all kinds of colors but wearing them to work screams; I rather be at home with my feet prompt up and watching cartoons.

## Friday's for jeans day

Everyone loves jeans because the feel is very relaxing and enjoyable to wear during the day. When most companies allow jeans day, the employees are always gong-ho for the workday. Wearing jeans is a sure way to preserve good interpersonal relations with employees and a unique way to encourage high team productivity. The focus of the company primary objective is the main initiative and while reaching the goal being comfortable is a major factor in reaching this target. An overview of the acceptable types of jeans are in order to comply with the company attire policy:

- *Blue Jeans.* The common selection of jeans mostly worn with a colored shirt to display a nice neat appearance and sustaining the conformability. Most name brands are worn from Polo to FUBU.

- *Colored Jeans.* An often selection to be different but still in style and acceptable attire from yellow to dark hunter green, the jeans are the right tint color and ironed.

- *Jean skirts.* A wonderful way to bring some flare and looking great during the workday many colors are available that can be matched with a pleasing top. For this type of attire selection, stockings need to be worn to comply with most companies' policies. The shoes can be either tennis shoes with socks or a type of shoe that is comfortable that no socks are required—rather stockings are used.

- *Jeans Jumper Dress.* A nice ensemble that is a one piece that is so comfortable and really professional if the right one is selected. The size should not be tight but roomy and comes to your ankles. The individual will wear a shirt with sleeves underneath the jumper to comply with the company policy when the jumper is sleeveless.

- *Jeans Jumper Pants.* Most companies might not allow this selection but worn with the correct accessories the attire can be acceptable. I will advise to stick with blue jeans and stay away from color jeans jumper pants. Underneath wear a nice starch shirt that color coordinates with the jeans appropriately. Yellow, red, or tan colors are a nice choice that flatters the casual look and still present a professional and neat appearance. Top off the look with tennis shoes that have a low heal and thin socks.

The above outline is a great overview of what is acceptable in Corporate America. There are many selections, however, the key is choosing wisely.


## Friday Jean's Day

*What is not allowed?*

Most will be surprised to know that individuals usually make bad choices in choosing their jeans. The individual seems to get caught up in the notion of comfortablitiy and ends up not making a good choice. Below are the most no—no's in wearing jeans in Corporate America when the company has designated Jeans Day.

Jeans that are not allowed or not appropriate in most companies:

- *Capri Jeans.* No jeans that come to your ankles and that are cut off presenting a fuzzy edge at the end of each leg. Besides not being allowed in most companies, this appearance screams un-professionalism.

- *Thin white jeans.* These types of jeans are so thin, and with the color being white it will showcase the individual's underwear or anything else you really don't want anyone to see. It screams bad taste.

- *Tight jeans.* Most jeans that fit well when a selection is made based on the individual size; however, I am referring to tight jeans that are so relevant that lines are seen from the individual back thighs. Allowing for the difficult to bend down, getting up comfortably, or even walking normally should be a sure sign of not making this your selection for the workday. With this selection, it appears that no conscious effort was made to make sure you are looking professional and that is not the message you should make.

- *Baggy jeans.* On the weekend, the baggy jeans will be nice a selection for going to the mall, grocery story, or garage sale. However, the business environment when competition is fierce the individual needs to choose wisely. Baggy jeans imply that causal is a day of really being comfortable to the point of almost placing on slides or beach sandals. I am not referring to one size bigger that is loose—but rather not too loose. I am talking about overly loose jeans that at times you will have to pull up the jeans during the workday. This is a no—no.

~ ~ ~

Incorporating this practice in choosing the appropriate attire will present a professional image, and in the long run you will feel great that you are an effective player focusing on the company's initiative.

# CHAPTER 6

# Hair Attitudes

Nichel Anderson:

*"I twisted the two strand hair strand dangling in front of my face as my manager chatted away trying to avoid the glory of my natural Nubian hair. I smiled and beamed brightly exposing my confidence in myself as well as in my blessed attribute that my creator had given me; my naturally curly right hair. My manager returned the smile as if he was given the insight to know it as well."*

I used to dread my hair appointments when a perm was needed. Years later I decided to not use chemicals anymore, and decided to focus on my true beauty. Others didn't join my bandwagon but then there were some who did. Here I will provide some insight into Corporate America dealing with hairstyles and an effective way to wearing hair styles while working in a corporate environment.

**The Texture:**

First thing first. We range from many different ethnic backgrounds and our genetics are key to what we are born with to project an image. I, for example, have natural cotton soft hair that provides a different look than someone who doesn't have the same texture. Most individuals either have my type of texture or a more straighter look that are capable of different styles on a person. Either fullness or limpness we have to learn to work with what we have been given, and we should seek professional help to achieve a more acceptable appearance.

\*\*\*

**The Style:**

The first measure in accomplishing a professional look is being neat in the choice of style. We all know that at times getting to the hairstylist is hard with our hectic schedule. Try to implement ways to keep it tame to project a doable style and look with accessories or a manageable cut. There are many styles that are acceptable to prevent any unwanted bad impressions. The key is not overly doing the look but emphasizing what you do have to reach your goal; a professional look while the acceptance of diversity is present at your company. Also, you might want to seriously consider looking into feedback from a hair professional and use the feedback to open up new opportunities in expressing a great look. You can also check out hair magazines that provide an array range of styles, in addition, the articles and pictures provide effective ways to being in style and looking professional with any hair texture. Furthermore, you should find products that enhance your look to present the finest qualities for your hair. Stay away from the extreme rather emphasize clean, sharp, and neat styles that encourage your wonderful smile and a great successful attitude.

The final keynote to remember here is that you don't want attention to be primarily centered on your hair but rather on your intelligence and dedication to the company.

\*\*\*

## The Acceptance:

Nobody wants to feel that they don't belong because they are different from their counterparts. At times this experience happens, it is up to you to overcome with confidence. In addition, it is up to others to acceptance those that are different from them either by race, religion or culture identity.

\*\*\*

## Mastering Diversity:

Being kind to those who are different from you is crucial to not only developing effective interpersonal skills with co-worker but also understanding culture. There are countless times where co-workers express bias and ignorance to different hair texture—not the style but the texture that symbolizes difference. Learning to accept that diversity exists prominently in Corporate America will produce a productive work environment. Positive and constructive criticism is one thing but sarcastic unprecedented looks and comments are another that does not unify the team.

~ ~ ~

Lastly, the important note is understanding that you are a player on a team bringing your expertise and professionalism. Therefore, the styles you choose represent a prestige appearance to establish a message of success. The texture allows you to be creative in what was given to you to represent in a positive light.

# CHAPTER 7

# Marketing Tips to Move Up the Corporate Ladder

Nichel Anderson:

*"I shook the managers hand and he smiled back at me with the ease that he just hired the right person for the job."*

Life will open doors for you but it is up to you to step through and make things happen. An effective resume can get you that interview to showcase your expertise and dedication to work hard for the company. A resume is your ticket to achieve a great opportunity of a successful career.

## Making Your Resume Stand Out From The Rest

The job market is a very competitive avenue to stand out from all the rest. How does your resume succeed in getting a call from the hiring manager of the company you wish to be employed with? Your resume should present, professionalism, correct spelling, punctuation, experience related to the open position, the data presented in an order, and exceptional references. Many individuals go to a professional resume writer who can deliver these attributes at a costly price. There is also resume software to assist those who wish to tackle the task themselves. If you fit in this category follow the below technique to making your resume stand out.

**An Effective Resume:**

a. Your resume should be no more than two pages and any additional pages are additional information for review, i.e. cover letter and references.

b. Have an objective preceding your name and address to provide the hiring manager a quick overview of what your goals are for the future in the related field.

c. Next, a breakdown of your experiences with other companies who provide the time your were there, your title, and keep your duties not overly detailed but short enough to still give a concise idea what you duties you performed at that establishment.

d. If all possible list jobs that closely match to the current opening position you are applying for now, the hiring managers always pay close attention to duties and positions that relates to the position trying to be filled—and that is what you want…to catch their attention.

e. Keep the number of jobs to a minimum since you only have two pages to professionally present your experience on paper. The norm is 3 to 4 listings.

f.  List your education and provide any diplomas or certifications that you have received or in the process of receiving. The year of completion is optional but not necessary.

g.  Also have a technical section that will provide the employer your technical expertise. In these days, everyone needs to at least be computer friendly and manage email.

h.  Lastly, your references should reflect individuals who not only will speak highly on your behalf, but an additional plus are those who are in the same industry.

~ ~ ~

**Professional Resume**

Lets review a professional resume and the key points presented:

\*\*\*\*\*\*\*\*\*\*\*\*\*\*\*\*\*\*\*\*\*\*\*\*\*\*\*\*\*\*\*\*\*\*\*\*\*\*\*\*\*\*\*\*\*\*\*\*\*\*\*\*\*\*\*\*\*\*\*\*\*\*\*\*\*\*\*\*\*\*\*\*\*\*\*\*

# Nichel Anderson

*Objective:* An opportunity to utilize my analytical experience to further my personal and professional growth in Corporate America.

*Summary of Qualifications: I am familiar with providing financial analysis and reporting to the Manager of Financial Analysis. I held the responsibilities of conducting exceptionally integrity monthly accounting closing balance sheet reconciliation's and the preparation of financial targets, forecasts and the performance measurement. In addition, my communication skills with upper management is conducted in a productive, diplomatic, and always in a professional way.*

Experience:    Aug. 2001—Current    Unknown    Unknown City, State

**Medicare Financial Analyst**

• Balanced and reconciled daily Ocala Medical Center and Ft. Walton Beach Medical Center General Ledger accounts receivable contractual adjustments too Medicare remittance summary on Excel spreadsheets. Exported documents from Document Direct through Docu-Analizer to Excel workbooks. Responsible for month-end closing for hospitals by reconciling the general ledger totals and remittance advice.

• Deciphered if Medicare overpaid on credit balances and performed necessary account fixes of P-lines, RD lines, IZ lines in order to fix Patient Accounting database as well as the Log and Collections databases. Noted findings and handlings of accounts in the Credit Refund Tool and the Web Refund Tool.

• Reconciled hospitals Bad Dept accounts weekly onto an Excel spreadsheet. Performed Month-End reconciliation of remaining Bad Debt and RA advice to accumulations of daily totals onto month end balancing Excel sheet. In addition, worked the collections series, discrepancy reports, and the CPAJ07 contractual differences report weekly.

Apr. 1999—Aug. 2001          Unknown       Unknown City, State

**Recovery Savings Analyst**

• Researching unsolicited and solicited refund checks to determine the reason for receipt and correct resolution. Sending for deposits, voiding claims, ordering batches through Outlook, re-mailing correspondences. Updating ROCS system and documenting check research on ROS and Excel. Performing CMS transactions for traditional checks to be deposited. Knowledge and handling DRG/Pricer for division with extensive calculation of benefits.

• Contacting members/providers through telephone or written correspondences. Referred updated contract information from provider relations to the LOFA and GPS departments. Extensive knowledge of PII system of processing claims and recalculation of claims.

**•September, 1996—April, 1999**      Unknown      Unknown City, State

**Senior Claims Examiner**

• Handling a large volume of HMO and PPO claims from providers on a production type environment. Primarily spent time in the Commercial Claims Unit before transferring to the Senior-Care Claims Division. Assisting on aged reports and personal on-hand reports, handling of PMDS calls, in which, recalculation was needed on previously process claims. Dealt with faxes as haste issues from customer service representatives and the plan coordinator.

Oct. 1995 to Sept. 1996      Unknown      Unknown City, State

**Billing Account Representative:**

• Assisting patients with their accounts. Procedure entry, posting payments of patients and insurance companies. Reading explanation of benefits and doing adjustments, refilling claims, and some coding that led to the usage of the CPT, ICD 9 book, and dealing with different modifiers.

• Typing up letters for review or appeal of a denied claim or a low allowable payment from insurance companies. Follow up with HMO, PPO, and IPA with extensive reading of aging reports.

• Knowledge of major insurance companies payment methods and filing deadlines: Medicare, Medicaid, AvMed, BCBS, Anthem and PCA. Extensive data entry and research work.

Apr. 1994 to Oct. 1995       Unknown     Unknown City, State

**Billing Account Representative:**

• Creating patients accounts and updating patient's incorrect addresses. Posting procedure, payments from Pathologists, Dermatologists reports, and balancing patients accounts. Follow up work with HMO, PPO, and IPA's with current and aging accounts.

• Knowledge of major insurance companies; Blue Cross Blue Shield, Medicare, Medicaid, AvMed, Aetna. Very extensive analytical skills with exceptional computer entry experience in an accuracy environment.

**Education:**          *Sandalwood Senior High School*
Unknown City, State

*Florida Community College of Jacksonville*
Unknown City, State

*Memorial Hospital*
Unknown City, State
*Certificate in Medical Terminology*

*Health Insurance Association of America*
Unknown City, State
*Currently half way in completion of a certified HIA designation*

**Technical Skills:** Windows 98, Windows Millennium 2000, Microsoft Word 2000, Outlook, Excel 98, PowerPoint Office 97, Document Direct, DocuAnalizer and the Internet. Ten by touch, Medical Manager software, 50wpm, and knowledge of CRT with 10,000 data entry keystrokes.

## REFERENCES:

Pamela King
Division Manager at Aetna US Healthcare
Anytown, USA
555.555.0000

~~~~~~~~~~~~~~~~~~~

Jermaine Ceasar-Porter
Recalculation Specialist at Aetna US Healthcare
Anytown, USA
555.555.4000

~~~~~~~~~~~~~~~~~~~

Bridgett Anderson
Supervisor at Vistakon
Anytown, USA
555.555.1000

**Freelance Resume**

Another resume that to give highlights of your talents if you are more technical or a freelancer, try the below approach:

\*\*\*\*\*\*\*\*\*\*\*\*\*\*\*\*\*\*\*\*\*\*\*\*\*\*\*\*\*\*\*\*\*\*\*\*\*\*\*\*\*\*\*\*\*\*\*\*\*\*\*\*\*\*\*\*\*\*\*\*\*\*\*\*\*\*\*\*\*\*\*\*\*\*\*\*

# Nichel Anderson

**Objective:** *Providing influential writing services to promote a business focus initiative.*

**Experience:**

2001-Current        Unknown        Unknown City, State

**Book Reviewer**

• Reviews non-fiction, fictional, and motivational books for African-American Literary Book Club; an online bookstore.

• Critiquing poetry collections of new or well known published poets to be published on AALBC.com site.

• Writing an in-depth profile of the literary content with a rating for visitors to the site, in which, AALBC.com receives over one million hits a month.

2001-Current        Unknown        Unknown City, State

**Content Manager**

• Built website for client, Melvin L. Mitchell, FAIA, professor and director of architecture and planning program at Morgan State University in Baltimore.

• Providing weekly content for the promotion of his book, monitoring the message boards, proofread and verifies related links to post on his site.

• Publicists; Organizing his book tour, setting up lectures and book signings at notable Universities as well as local TV and Radio stations.

• Wrote his book proposal and marketing plan.

2001-Current              Unknown              Unknown City, State

**Reading & Literature Community Manager**

• Provide weekly literature content to over 3000 members.

• Oversee 1500 editors, review, and proofread articles for the featured slot.

• Post bulletins in the literary world, polls, moderate the forum, and plan events.

• Communicate effectively to senior project manager, editor in chief on improvements to the communities. Answers visitors, members, and editors questions. Post updated news in the literary.

2000-2001              Unknown              Unknown City, State

**Freelance Writer**

• Proofreader

• Technology Article: Intellitech Inc.

• Architecture Article: Uarchitopia.

• Book Reviews: On related topics of technology, construction, interior design, development and the arts.

2000-Current                    Unknown                    Unknown City, State

**Contributing Editor**

• Editor of Harlem Renaissance topic.

• Providing biweekly articles on the Harlem Renaissance with discussion by essays and reviews of works by famous literary and poets.

• Obtaining new links to sources related to the Harlem Renaissance.

1996-2001                       Unknown                    Unknown City, State

**Newsletter Editor**

• Started the first newsletter of the diversity network based in the Jacksonville office for the AAEN members and employees.

• Articles relating to technology, professional development, and networking.

• Develop and written the newsletter proposal.

1995-2001                       Unknown                    Unknown City, State

**Nonfiction/Fiction Author**

• Mitsray. Part 1 & 2, a nonfiction novel.

• Bahamas, a fiction novel, The Very Thought Of You, a short story.

1995-2001                       Unknown                    Unknown City, State

**Resume Writer**

• Writing professional resumes from scratch or touch ups.

• Cover letters with salary requirements.

**Education**

1999-2001                    Harcourt Learning Direct Scranton, PA
                             Certified Freelance Writer

**Websites Sites I have designed and managing:**

*http://melvinmitchell.writernetwork.com*
*http://www.suite101.com/readingcenter*
http://www.suite101.com/welcome.cfm/harlem_renaissance

**Technical**

Windows Millennium 2000, HTML Coding, PowerPoint, Excel, Word
2000.

# REFERENCES

Kathleen Ettienne
President of Blacklines Magazines
2001 Newkirk Avenue Ste 7-D
Anytown, USA 12226
Phone: 555.555.8000
Fax: 555.555.1900

~~~~~~~~~~~~~~~~~~~~~~~~~~~~~~~

Melvin L. Mitchell, FAIA
Director and Professor of Morgan State University
Vice President of the Eastern Region of NOMA
National Organization of Minority Architects
413 Van Buren St. NW
Anytown, USA 25181
Phone: 555.555.1000
Work: 555.555.2000

~~~~~~~~~~~~~~~~~~~~~~~~~~~

Roxianne Moore
Senior Managing Editor at Suite101.com
P.O.B 1077
Anytown, USA 15044
Phone/Fax: 555.555.1200
Email Address: Roxmoore@usa.com

~~~~~~~~~~~~~~~~~~~~~~~~~~~

Rina Khosla
Senior Project Coordinator at Suite101.com
210-1122 Mainland Street
Anytown, Canada V6B-5L1
Phone: 555.555.1400 ext.106
Email Address: Rina@usa.com

**An Effective Cover Letter:**

Many employers will request a cover letter with your resume. The potential employee must present a concise and professional cover letter in order to restate their expertise outline in the resume. First, the individual must provide the needed information the employer is requesting which mostly will require your salary requirements, the desired position, and why in so many words you are the perfect candidate. Secondly, the individual has to present the pre-said requests in a way that do not project your focus is soley on money and rather than the company objectives. You might be surprised how many cover letters that scream what their primary focus is set on. Thirdly, the individual will have to end the letter to re-enforce his/her commitment to the company initiatives in order to reach the company's goals and prompting the hiring manager to call for an interview.

Below are two different ways to effectively write a cover letter that provides the main requirements an employer asks in seeking new hires:

**Cover Letter #1:**

Debra S. Nanton
2137 Lutbend Lane
Unknown, State

Bill Daley
Tellicom Inc.
Human Resources Department
777 North West 79th Avenue Room #102
Unknown, State

Dear Mr. Daley:

I was referred by Joe White to send my resume to your attention, regarding a position as a Service Technician. I am an expert technician with 20 years of experience to offer Tellicom Inc.

My recent experience was a Network II Technician, at Lolles Bank. In addition, I was a troubleshooter for many prominent telephone companies. I also am experienced with different in-house and mainframe computers. As a Service Technician with Tellicom Inc.,

I would bring focus on quality and efficiency to your organization.

I look forward to an opportunity to discuss my qualifications in an interview.

Sincerely,
Debra S. Nanton

**Cover Letter #2:**

Stacy Williamson
7521 Sutton Road
Unknown, State
904.555.1111

Human Resources Manager
Taylor Technology Services
Human Resources Department
355 Bullington Street
Unknown, State

Dear Human Resources Manager:

I am a dedicated employee with strong analytical skills that will be a great asset to your company initiatives. Over my many years at major corporations, I have mastered the ability to present my technical ability to excel in my job duties. Currently, my range is $47,100 a year where I am a System Analyst for multiple clients. My recent experience as an analyst, both at the current company and the previous business entity, I was continually commented on how I resolved the issues that came up and reported the results with effective communication to my immediate supervisor. Finally, my many years in Corporate America has challenged me to work with different specialized individuals to provide me a rich perspective of my professional career.

I look forward to an opportunity to discuss my qualifications in an interview.

Sincerely,
Stacy Williamson

## Writing A Biography:

It is always wise to have a biography available along with your resume. Most companies after the initial contact with you would like to get to know something about your well rounded life. This measure develops a more interpersonal relationship before a job offer is presented and a biography along with your resume will provide the interviewer and other hiring personnel—a more in-depth knowledge of a potential future employee. Start with your education, and then you should proceed by providing any pertinent positions you held with a brief description of the duties. In addition, you should provide any additional experiences and accomplishments that will not only highlight your skills but your personality.

## Nichel Anderson's Biography

Nichel attended Alabama A&M University, in Huntsville Alabama, for a Marketing degree. Nichel's hobbies are African-American History, traveling and writing—which is her passion. Nichel has written seven novels ranging from fiction, non-fiction, and short stories. In the very near future she plans to self-publish her first novel.

Nichel's professional career was previously at Aetna US Healthcare, in which, Nichel was a Recovery Savings Analyst. She was on the Executive Committee Board of the Aetna African-American Employee Network focusing on Diversity in Corporate America. Nichel's agenda was the Professional Development and Networking initiatives, and she was the Editor of the network newsletter. Currently, she is employed with HCA, The Healthcare Company, as a Discrepancy Analyst for multiple hospitals. In her spare time, she writes articles for different professional periodicals and is the publicist for Melvin Mitchell, FAIA, Director and Associate Professor of the Architecture Program at Morgan State University for his newly released book titled:

*"The Crisis of the African-American Architect:*
*Conflicting Cultures of Architecture and (Black) Power"*

Nichel built, designed, and is the Content Manager for Mr. Mitchell's official literary website. She is also planning his book tour with location, dates, and times located at the Mr. Mitchell's official website.

~ ~ ~

## A More Personal Approach: Biography

I often have to use a more personal approach in writing my biography and always get positive response. Try the below method to achieve the message you wish to accomplish that is geared to a specific subject, i.e. books or writing.

## Nichel's Personal Approach Biography:

Books are my ultimate favorite pass time, for they provide a new awareness of a world I might not have experienced. I particularly enjoy reading quality African-American authored literature, not only for the cultural relationship but also due to the richness of flavor. The ability to reach out and touch your heart, in order, for you to listen to what the message is being relayed…moves one's soul. I have been reading since my very early teens, and it has tremendously increased while I attended college. My preferred interest has changed which was a result of my intense hunger of African-American subjects. The need to feel connected, loved, honored, and most importantly respected—fueled my passion of reading.

Poetry has always been a form of art that I cherish when listening to a poet or reading their passage in a book. It unbinds the tangle of one's emotion and releases their fears, guilt, and misunderstandings…to the freedom of expression. I look for pure love in this form of creativity. I am the author of seven books ranging from non-fiction, fiction, and short stories as well as some poetry. I was previously the newsletter Editor for Aetna US Healthcare African-American Employee Diversity Network. Now I am the Editor of the topic the Harlem Renaissance at Suite101.com writing bi-weekly articles, providing related links, books and poetry reviews, and biographies on the most influential black folks in African-American history. I admit, I love the Harlem Renaissance because it is filled with black love of self…resulting in the best exceptional creativity of art expression from the literary masterminds, poets, painters, sculptures, dancers, musicians, architects, and the political thinkers.

I am also a freelance writer for periodicals ranging from different topics of architecture, technology, and business profiles. My newest published articles are in Blacklines Magazine owned by three black women architects in Brooklyn, New York. I am the publicist and website content manager for Melvin L. Mitchell, FAIA, the director and associate professor of the architecture institute program at Morgan State University.

My Motto:

*I choose each day to Succeed!*

Favorite Quotes That I Live By:

*"If you have no confidence in self you are twice
defeated in the race of life. With confidence you have
won even before you have started," Marcus Garvey*

*"You may write me down in history with your bitter,
twisted lies, You may trod me in the very dirt but
still, like dust, I'll rise," Maya Angelou*

## References Letters

Having an effective reference letter is a sure way to guarantee of being a runner up for the open position. Whenever you had a great relationship with upper management, you need to ask for a reference letter that you keep for future use when you are about to or will be looking for other employment. Most of the time it works well to ask for one when you are about to leave the company or if you are performing additional work outside of your current day job i.e., freelance work, etc. Below I have presented two different methods and ways an effective reference letter can enhance your career:

**Reference Letter #1:**

November 23, 2xxx

To whom it may concern:
Re: Sheri Brown

Sheri has worked remotely for me at Holleson.com from April 2000, until the present as a Web Page Manager for Holleson Inc.

Her duties are to operate the web page by managing and sometimes creating, the content that will be featured. She has exceeded all of my expectations. Sheri has taken the initiative to find out what the visitors are looking for and are interested in. As a result, the official Holleson, Inc. website page hits Synopsis From the Publisher are steadily increasing. Sheri is extremely skilled at working independently and is always able to meet or beat her deadlines.

Her skills and work ethic will be an asset in whatever job career she chooses. I wish Sheri all the best in her future endeavors. Please feel free to contact me if you have any questions. My phone number is 555.121.2110 ext. 202 and my email address is bobby@holleson.com.

Yours sincerely,

Bobby Witherson
Senior Project Manager
Holleson, Inc.

**Reference Letter #2:**

July 10, 2xxx
Rick YaSinge
Corrella Magazine
Executive Director of Editorial

To Whom It May Concern:
Subject: Todd Anderson

Todd Anderson has been an Editor at Corrella Magazine since February 2xxx. In this capacity, he performs copy editing services, and writes articles, reviewing books, and presenting insightful essays for the magazine. He also searches the World Wide Web for sites and articles relating to his assign department focus, monitors and facilitates assignments to Writer and finds news-related items for his department.

Editor, Todd must maintain her own column, which generally requires at least 2 years of editorial and effective writing skills. He has done an admirable job in preparing an attractive and informative topic department focus page that has enormously increased sales for the magazine.

In addition, Todd recently began administering our "Editor's Corner," a position for which I recommended him. As a manager for the "Editor's Corner," Todd chooses which fan letter to focus on and feature amongst more than 7000 subscribed readers on a wide range of topics. He also chooses an event or topic to spotlight, monitors responses on selected discussions, and posts polls to survey subscribed readers.

Since coming on board as both an editor and a manager, Todd has done excellent work for us. He brings both competence and enthusiasm to the job, and I can sincerely recommend him to an editorial position at your company.

Sincerely,
Rick YaSing
Senior Managing Editor
Corrella Magazine

~ ~ ~

The key-note to remember is sustaining great relationships so that when you do decide to move up the corporate ladder—you can show your potential manager that you are a team player with profound experience.

## Mastering The Interview Process

Your opportunity to get an offer for a job at the company, the interview is a sure way the employer will determine if you are a suitable person for the position. In succeeding in being effective for your first interview and any possible subsequent interview, the individual must be well prepared. Being prepared separates the successful candidates from the not so successful candidates. The employer will surely appreciate the alertness, knowledgeable, and experienced interaction of conversation during the interview.

## Before the interview incorporate the following:

- Remember the contact person you are to ask for on the day of your interview.

- Learn all you can about the company, visit their official website, ask co-workers or friends what they know or heard about the company.

- The night before, make sure you have an answer to the usual questions the employer asks i.e., Why did you apply with us? What are your current job duties? How do you think they relate to the present position you wish to fill? What was the most positive thing you enjoyed at your present employment establishment? What is the least thing that you enjoyed about your present employment? Why are you leaving your current employment?

- Don't forget to wear something that emphasizes a smart and professional image, so try colors that are dark—i.e. black or navy blue. Make sure the outfit is wrinkle free with coordinating shoes to match. Try not to over do with any jewelry; instead, keep it simple. For men, a nice watch or simple bracelet and for women, a pair of pearls.

Incorporating these measures will guarantee a well-received response with a potential employer. The applicant must demonstrate confidence, professionalism, and experience, and the applicant's image must deliver these attributes in a nutshell.

## Mastering The Interview Process cont.

During the interview can be very intimating for most and especially when in todays market, the panel interview process is the preferred method of choice by companies. Learning not only being prepared but calm and relaxed is the key to a successful interview process no matter what technique is being used. Below are some useful and pertinent tips in succeeding in getting an offer to fill the open position.

**The day of the interview:**

- Bring two copies of your resume along with references with updated contact numbers and addresses.

- Arrive at the interview destination at least 10 minutes early to not only gather your nerves but to make sure you are able to find the location and where you are having the interview.

- Be prepared for a strong handshake from the interviewee. A strong one emphasis not only strength, however, but also strength in yourself as the right person for the job. In addition, a good short squeeze with eye contact will demonstrate a professional image to a potential employer.

- Once seated always keep a good posture and your hands directly in front of you clasped together—that will exemplify an alert person.

- Have an opening statement due to most interviewers will say something to encourage a response to get a feel for your personality upfront. For example, a great statement that emphasizes a particular fact of the company is a sure winner.

- Keep your answers on target to the question being asked and remember to give eye contact to the interviewer or interviewees if is a panel of hiring managers doing the interview.

- After the interview, an individual should send a thank you note and a follow up call to see if the position has been filled or not. Allow at least 3 days after your interview to follow up.

## The Tools Of The Trade Towards Success:

Managing your career is so much easier than forty years ago due to the wide range of electronics that makes our lives easier. Either from techno gadets or office software, the important point to remember is to find out what is available and use the gadgets or software to your advantage.

### *Managing The Power Of The Pocket PC*

On the go with a dozen objectives to do and little time to spare—sound familiar? In today's world no matter where you are located at on the globe, time is of the essence and having a manageability tool that can produce high productive results will make you a winner. Most individuals are too busy to browse the local computer stores, or pay attention during lunch and miss out on the conversations going on about the latest manageability tools on the market. However, it only takes a moment to gather the information of what you need and what you don't need, to get back on track of managing your business agendas.

The newest mobile device for workaholics is NEC's pocket PC, the *MobilePro P300*. It is smooth and thin enough to fit in your coat pocket or purse and is packed with the highest technology in the field. The slick gray color and smooth finish is like a brand new Jaguar with stylish buttons for easy maneuvering and navigation. NEC's first personal digital assistant, the *MobilePro P300*, is based on Microsoft's powerful Pocket PC 2002 operating system. The *MobilePro P300* has a custom utility that lets users synchronize email, swap data, and back up files to corporate servers by using a wireless card; however, you must obtain a service provider on your own.

You can update your P300 almost anywhere. NEC offers a one-day rapid exchange service, in case your P300 has an untimely accident. You also get Westek's robust Clear Vue file viewer and Arcsoft's PhotoBase, a handy, simple application for viewing and managing digital images. In addition, a silver metal case is included that truly complements the corporate theme of business-oriented individuals striving for success.

It is possible to accidentally press the dedicated dictation button, generating a series of short audio files, which can lead to some interesting experiences. The P300's color screen can display over 60,000 colors. The unit's combination of active-screen lighting and a reflective backing provides an easy way to view the contents on the screen from indoors or outdoors in bright sunlight. The front panel displays the maneuvering buttons that are surrounded by the four standard task buttons under the display, and a simple four-way cursor ring frames a tiny speaker. Scrolling can also be accomplished by rolling a dial located on the PDA's edge, and by firmly pressing it in order to make your selections. The P300's sync cradle has both USB and serial ports to make it compatible with most PCs. The unit comes with a USB cable and a serial converter if you so choose.

The P300's memory options include both Compact Flash and a Secure Digital socket, with half of its 64MB of Ram residing on an included Secure Digital media card. The only feature that didn't rise to par was when music played through the speaker. It didn't provide a crisp or electrifying sound; rather, it was raspy to say the least.

The P300, retailing at $599.99, is a great price for the many features that it offers. You can also check out comparable models like the HP Jornada 565 or the Toshiba E570 in order to help you choose the best mobile device for your needs. In today's world of business, we must gather all the essentials that will help us to excel in our chosen careers. For this is our *passion* and what drives us to want to expand the normal work hours and accomplish the set business objectives. While during the weekends, or holidays, or even on vacation we still need to be accessible to the corporate home office, and the technology today makes this transition accessible. After hours away from the office at a distant location, the business-minded individual will be more able to achieve business goals with a mobile device.

I recently read an excerpt by an executive of how he often checked his Pocket PC for updates on an important client case while vacationing in Bermuda. Of course, the wife and kids were away for a moment, but nonetheless, it didn't interfere with his vacation to have quick access to information, ready for him to tap into within seconds. This is the advancement of technology, which allows more and more extended hours outside of the norm to use efficiently and effectively. In addition, these small palm personal computers are for the driven business minded individual to explore new worlds with a simple *press here* and a *scroll there*. It keeps you connected. It allows you to have access to those urgent board meeting minute notes, when the meeting was just announced while you were on a much-needed weekend getaway.

Most importantly, it keeps you well organized. With all the many tasks to do in a given day and how the time seems to just slip away, a person needs to get organized and stay connected. A Pocket PC delivers that in a nutshell; no matter if you finally decide to get one or which one you ultimately choose. The main point is to get a Pocket PC if you so desire to excel in your chosen industry. Read up on the newest trends and compare them with what your needs are, and the Pocket PC will be there, waiting to be tailored to your needs. There are many different books to assist in getting familiar with your Pocket PC, and you should take the time not only to read the manual, but also to read books that highlight the extraordinary features of this fast-selling device. One in particular is by David Pogue *"Palm Pilot: The Ultimate Guide With CDROM, 2nd Edition."* It is the ultimate book about Palms, providing the very basics from built applications to text input to how hot-sync works. In addition, check out *"How To Do Everything With Your Palm Handheld,"* by Dave Johnson and Rick Broida. They have banded together to write a comprehensive guide to the basics of Palm usage.

Being well connected is the key to success in this new century of technology, and a person must be willing to meet the challenge to succeed in a goal-oriented focus. The technology companies are making these challenges easy for those that are willing to get focused, organized, and strive to success…even beyond office hours.

**Better Time Management Using Microsoft Outlook:**

We all need to prioritize our job duties. Using your PC to better manage your time is a good way to achieve this goal. By keying in data that you need to remember from a project deadline or getting that confirmation of your requested conference room:

*"Managing your PC gives you the cutting edge in the corporate world."*

Microsoft Outlook provides an excellent method of better time management. The calendar feature lets you choose from a 5-day format or a 7-day format that is set up like a column, which gives you some flexibility as to what your future days look like. You also have the option of a 31-day format that gives you a complete view of the month compared to a large desk calendar taking up your workspace.

Microsoft Outlook makes even the inexperienced user a pro; it's very friendly, letting you add an item or delete it with ease.

By clicking the calendar option to the left and choosing what day format you prefer you are on your way. Next, you just need to choose the month and the day of the event, appointment, or meeting and then type in the corresponding field with all the needed details of the occasion.

The benefits of Microsoft Outlook are great in regard to getting you more organized for your day or your upcoming agendas. A reminder memo pops up on your screen with a description of your agenda and will ask you if you wish to be reminded in 5 minutes or even longer. By using these features it will you save time on using sticky notes posted around your work area; Microsoft Outlook takes care of that for you with just a point and click. How you choose to use the different days of the week option is a personal preference. The important thing is trying the Microsoft Outlook Calendar to reap the rewards of organizing your time by documenting your work objectives.

The key in any work environment is taking a few moments to get familiarize with your office equipment. Who has the time with so many meetings, team projects, and conference calls? But if you want to be efficient and effective in your career, learning the tools to get you there is a must.

The best way to start is providing a set time during the week that will be focused entirely to learning the new tools of the trade of better manageability. Most companies have the previous versions of software, and you can use this method to your advantage. Many individuals know the shortcuts to the older version rather than the newest ones just out on the market. To a busy person like you, *time is everything.*

So with your set time to focus on clicking here and there, start asking around the office to your co-workers concerning their tips of advice prior to your allotted time to self-train. Write down the notes, draw arrows, draw images if you like that will help you remember what the person said to look for, and I promise that you will be off to a great start. Once you are ready to begin, keep your note pad for any new questions relating to what you wish to learn or questions that arise when you get stuck on something. If you really want to get the answer now and no one is around, then you should find the *"Help"* option for when you need a quick solution to your problem.

My favorite way of getting to know the software is that I first take a moment and simply look at the screen. We are so busy *doing* the task at hand to meet the company's business objectives that we hardly ever take the time to see everything the program has to offer. Many times, I do find new and wonderful tools with the program that end up making my job much easier. So take a moment and surf around with the different options, and use the *"Help"* option to ask questions relating to the task you wish to accomplish. Also, the software program Office Assistant is an excellent way of getting familiar with the program; having a companion while you surf around is not bad either.

In most programs, the Office Assistant will perform the preferred selected task if you ask. This option is neat and educational when we just can't find the place to click to perform our desired needed task; the assistant will perform it for you. So have fun and use your 15-minute break to discover the wonders of office technology, which will make you more marketable as you learn the most needed manageability tools in your office. You will be amazed what you find and end up discovering a new way to better manage your office objectives.

~ ~ ~

Lastly, an effective team player in Corporate America not only has the best resume, cover letters, biography page, reference letters, and experience on high-tech gadgets and software but also can adapt to change. When you can adapt to change, you are on a path towards success and great rewards. The path can be tricky and difficult at times, but you can make the journey. Learning to get along with all different personalities of co-workers and rising above any obstacles will allow you to move up the corporate ladder much faster than those that let their emotional state dictate their experiences. Understanding that this moment will change, as it always does, you will be a winner working for Corporate America during your journey towards success.

# Recommended Reading

The 7 Habits of Highly Effective People: Powerful Lessons in Personal Change

*Stephen R. Covey*
Retail Price: $14.00
Format: Paperback, 1st ed., 319 pp.
ISBN: 0671708635
Publisher: Simon & Schuster
Pub. Date: August 1990

**Synopsis From the Publisher**
Stephen R. Covey's incredibly successful book is a pathway to wisdom and power. It offers a revolutionary program to breaking the patterns of self defeating behavior that keep us from achieving our goals and reaching our fullest potential, and describes how to replace them with a principle-focused approach to problem solving. A revolutionary "principle-centered" program that will help put readers on the path to lasting personal satisfaction and achievement. From the Publisher In The 7 Habits of Highly Effective People, author Stephen R. Covey presents a holistic, integrated, principle-centered approach for solving personal and professional problems. With penetrating insights and pointed anecdotes, Covey reveals a step-by-step pathway for living with fairness, integrity, honesty, and human dignity—principles that give us the security to adapt to change

and the wisdom and power to take advantage of the opportunities that change creates.

~ ~ ~ ~ ~ ~ ~ ~ ~ ~ ~ ~ ~ ~

## Daily Reflections for Highly Effective People: Living the Seven Habits Everyday
*Stephen R. Covey*
Retail Price: $11.00
Format: Paperback, 1st ed., 368pp.
ISBN: 0671887173
Publisher: Simon & Schuster Trade Paperbacks
Pub. Date: February 1994

### Synopsis From the Publisher
The groundbreaking approach set forth in Covey's bestsellers The 7 Habits of Highly Effective People and Principle-Centered Leadership has helped millions attain personal fulfillment and professional success. Now he brings his unique wisdom to a daily reading format—an easy-to-use distillation of the Seven Habits.

## How to Develop Self-Confidence and Influence People by Public Speaking
*Dale Carnegie Selected by Dorothy Carnegie*
Our Price: $7.50
Format: Paperback
ISBN: 0671746073
Publisher: Simon & Schuster
Pub. Date: May 1976

**Synopsis From the Publisher**

Dale Carnegie shows you how to: Develop poise, Gain self-confidence, Improve your memory, Make your meaning clear, Begin and end a talk, Interest and charm your audience, Improve your diction, Win and argument without making enemies. How to Develop Self-Confidence and Influence People by Public Speaking also offers hundreds of practical and valuable tips on influencing the important people in your life: your friends, your customers, your business associates, your employers. The information in this book has been tested and used successfully by more than one million students in the world-famous Dale Carnegie Course in Effective Speaking and Human Relations.

---

**Little Book of Coaching: Motivating People to Be Winners**
*Kenneth H. Blanchard*
Retail Price: $16.00
Format: Hardcover, 128pp.
ISBN: 0066621038
Publisher: HarperCollins Publishers
Pub. Date: February 2001

**Synopsis From the Publisher**

A guide to using the author's landmark strategy for coaching, outlined in their book, Everyone's a Coach, distilling their experience down into one helpful acronym: COACH, Conviction-driven, Over-learning, Audible-Ready, Consistency, and Honesty-Based. Shows how to use these five parts of the essential strategy to become a winning coach. Annotation Instructive and inspirational, The Little Book of Coaching is the essential handbook that will teach you how to unleash excellence in anyone. In The Little Book of Coaching, Don Shula and Ken Blanchard highlight the qualities of effective leadership-convictions, practice, and the ability to change, consistency, and honesty-and show that these traits can indeed be transferred from the football field to the board room and even the family room. The result is a marvelously succinct book that can serve as a touchstone of guidance for any situation-and a perfect gift for anyone who wants to be a winner.

~~~~~~~~~~~~~~~~~~~~~

**Harvard Business Review on Effective Communication**
*Harvard Business Review*
Retail Price: $19.95
Format: Paperback, 224pp.
ISBN: 1578511437
Publisher: Harvard Business School Publishing
Pub. Date: July 1999

**Synopsis From the Publisher**
The Harvard Business Review Paperback Series is designed to bring today's managers and professionals the fundamental information they need to stay competitive in a fast-moving world. Here are the landmark ideas that have established the Harvard Business Review as required reading for ambitious business people in organizations around the globe. With topics that include how to run a successful meeting, change frontline employees' behavior, and build effective management teams, Harvard Business Review on Effective Communication offers useful tips for all businesspeople.

~~~~~~~~~~~~~~~~~~~~~

**Harvard Business Review on Managing People**
*Harvard Business Review*
Retail Price: $19.95
Format: Paperback, 288pp.
ISBN: 0875849075
Publisher: Harvard Business School Publishing
Pub. Date: January 1999

**Synopsis From the Publisher**
From managing diversity to exploring alternative workplaces to debunking myths about compensation, the topics covered in this collection address how to build organizations with judicious and effective systems for managing people.

**The Gifted Boss: How to Find, Create, and Keep Great Employees**
*Dale A. Dauten Designed by Cathryn S. Aison*
Retail Price: $20.00
Format: Hardcover, 109pp.
ISBN: 0688168779
Publisher: Morrow, William & Co
Pub. Date: May 1999

**Synopsis From the Publisher**
Do you want to have great employees, people who don't need to be managed and who make everyone around them work harder and raise the department to a higher standard? Try this one: How does freedom from management mediocrity and morons sound? Pretty good, right? In The Gifted Boss, you'll quickly learn that this is the first step to making your workplace "the best place for the best people to work." The rest will follow, as Dale Dauten demonstrates in this winning tale of a successful business executive who turns to an eccentric management sage for advice

on how to become a gifted boss. To learn how it's done, Dauten went in search of the best bosses in America. He found them running small businesses, managing departments and heading major corporations. In revealing their secrets, he may jolt your notions of working life. This is a book about the spiral of energy, creativity and friendship that is business at its best.

0-595-26818-8